Plots & Pans

The Book Club Cookbook

Plots & Pans

The Book Club Cookbook

The Swivel Collective

SUMACH PRESS

NATIONAL LIBRARY OF CANADA CATALOGUING IN PUBLICATION

Plots & pans: the book club cookbook/by the Swivel Collective.

Includes indexes.
ISBN 1-894549-20-1
1. Cookery. 2. Literary cookbooks. 3. Book clubs. I. Swivel
Collective. II. Title: Plots and pans.

TX714.P585 2002   641.5   C2002-903977-0

Artwork for invitations by Bob Pierce of the SWIVEL Collective
Edited by Ruth Pincoe with the assistance of Beth McAuley,
Natalie Muhina and Jackie Grandy
Design by Liz Martin

Printed and bound in Canada

Published by

SUMACH PRESS
1415 Bathurst St., Suite 202
Toronto, Ontario, Canada
M5R 3H8

www.sumachpress.com

CONTENTS

SECTION FOUR

ORGANIZING BOOK CLUB MEETINGS BY THEME

The Swivel Collective
Left to right – Top Row: Heather MacDonald,
Kerry Houlahan, Liz McCullough
Bottom Row: Joyce Thompson, Bob Pierce,
Sharon Cook, Jane Reid

PREFACE

The name of our book club — SWIVEL — is an acronym based on the name of a school where the original members once taught. The meaning of the letters has faded over time, although we occasionally argue about it. The book club format was originally used as a forum in which members from various departments in the school could meet to discuss books in a social setting that would differ from staff-room chat at lunch or the hilarity of a TGIF.

SWIVEL soon developed into a club with a regular membership, which has slowly moved beyond the founding school as teachers moved or retired. SWIVEL has now operated for more than sixteen years with three principles at its heart: to read (and debate) enjoyably, to socialize companionably and, above all, to eat fabulously. Today the SWIVEL Book Club is a group of twelve women and men who live and work in the Ottawa area. Many, now retired from careers in education, are avid gardeners, travellers and community volunteers. Their mutual delight in reading, discussion, cooking and eating inspired this collection.

Two years ago, someone suggested that we should gather together some of the best of the club's invitations and its tastiest recipes to create a cookbook for our own use. A group of seven members took on the cookbook project. When Sumach Press expressed an interest in the first draft, the group of seven became the SWIVEL Collective, the compilers responsible for *Plots & Pans*. The SWIVEL Collective is:

- BOB PIERCE, a retired teacher-librarian, who traces his SWIVEL lineage back to meeting number two, is the creative genius behind the beautiful, clever and inspiring invitations members receive to announce each book club meeting. He is also the humble two-fingered typist who has entered all the data in the first manuscript while keeping us all keen and focused on the *Plots & Pans* project. Chapter by chapter he was able to see the book in his mind's eye, helped guide the project to fruition with inspired creativity, and still managed to keep his sanity in spite of AutoFormatting.

- SHARON COOK, the only remaining charter member, is the club's equivalent of a whirling dervish. As well as carrying a full teaching load in the Faculty of Education at the University of Ottawa, she balances an active family life, manages to publish scholarly articles, has recently edited the award-winning *Framing Our Past: Canadian Women's History in the Twentieth Century* with two colleagues, as well as maintaining a remarkable sense of humour, which is exceeded only by her boundless energy.

- KERRY HOULAHAN, the youngest member of the group who often displays great courage in playing the Devil's Advocate at SWIVEL meetings, is not only club archivist but also an extremely active member of her school community. Her wonderful sense of humour will continue to be an asset as she takes responsibility for the rest of us in our dotage.

- HEATHER MACDONALD, who entered the profession after raising two young men, may never retire, but will always have read everything on topic and more, and be willling to debate all with gusto. No bombe is too big, no goat cheese too little, no recipe too daunting.

- ELIZABETH MCCULLOUGH annually hosts the final meeting of SWIVEL in her luxuriant garden, often using the delicate flowers to spice up a boring dish, surprise a dull item or create such delicacies as her elder-flower pancakes. A former teacher of Engish and always an avid gardener, Elizabeth does volunteer work in the horticultural community and at an elementary school, and has recently taken up "walking on water."

- JANE REID, recently retired and newly converted to golf, is also our resident gadabout. Jane's keen interest in travel literature is exceeded only by her own travels abroad to cavort with penguins or waltz with Matilda or defy local golf courses.

- JOYCE THOMPSON, whose interest in all things gourmet and literary makes her an avid supporter of the cookbook project whether field testing a recipe, searching for minutiae in her local library or burning the midnight oil writing chapter intros. Her irrepressible wit helps enliven many a meeting. Joyce is currently involved in teaching pre-service candidates in the Bachelor of Education Program at the University of Ottawa.

What a team!

ACKNOWLEDGEMENTS

The SWIVEL Collective is part of the larger SWIVEL Book Club, and to those members not directly involved in the cook book project, we extend our thanks for their support, for their many outstanding recipes which have found their way into this book, and for their patience as discussions have inevitably been rerouted to recipe-testing, design questions and deadlines. Trish and Rick Morgan, Lorna Miller, Heather Blackburn, Kerry Callan-Jones, Nancy O'Connor and Eileen Woolsey: thank you; we promise to confine our discussions to other peoples' books in future.

The recipes in this cookbook come from a multitude of sources: some are adapted from cookbooks, newspapers and magazines, some by way of friends and family. As often as possible we have indicated the source but, inevitably, some recipes have passed through so many hands that the original source has been lost. The recipes in *Plots & Pans* represent sixteen years of trading the best-tasting recipes that have appeared at our SWIVEL gatherings — the ones that evoke the universally heard comment at communal gatherings: "Ooooh, this is soooo good! Can I have the recipe?"

The SWIVEL Collective appreciates the generosity and kindness with which we have felt supported throughout the production of this book. In particular, we thank Kevin O'Brien for lending his expertise in computer applications to this project, and for his willingness to help with formatting challenges of a bewildering range and depth. Pam Collacott has served as an inspiration and as a source of fine cooking through her celebrated workshops. We are grateful for the permission to use her recipes for Lemon Curd and Bread Pudding with Whiskey Sauce. We also thank Pat Staton who provided encouragement and support, and Ruth Pincoe for her outstanding editing of the manuscript. Without the unwavering enthusiasm and skills of Beth McAuley and Liz Martin of Sumach Press, this project would likely have remained only a book club discussion topic.

This volume is offered in memory of a valued and much-missed member of SWIVEL, Irene Corkill.

Introduction

BUILDING A SUCCESSFUL BOOK CLUB

"What is the use of a book," thought Alice, "without pictures or conversations?"

LEWIS CARROLL,
ALICE'S ADVENTURES IN WONDERLAND, 1865

ABOUT THIS BOOK

SWIVEL has operated for sixteen years with three principles at heart: to read and debate enjoyably, to socialize companionably and, above all, to eat fabulously. This book – *Plots & Pans* — is based on these same principles and has three goals:

- to provide examples of books, authors and themes around which book club meetings can be organized;
- to share recipes for some of the wonderful dishes created and enjoyed by members of SWIVEL;
- to communicate our enthusiasm for the world of book clubs in hopes of motivating others to organize their own circles of enjoyment.

A book club guide should offer reading lists, discussion questions and suggestions about organizing club activities. A cookbook should provide recipes. This book does both, and we hope that — like a rich béchamel sauce or a fine anthology of poetry — its whole will exceed the sum of its parts. In our book club, SWIVEL, we meet to eat good food and to discuss good books. For well over a decade our members have shared thousands of dishes and hundreds of titles. We eat to read, and we read to eat; the blend has been magical.

Each chapter opens with a menu. Most of the recipes are simple (to allow more time for reading), portable and creative, and call for ingredients that are readily available

---

RECIPE FOR A SUCCESSFUL BOOK CLUB

- Up to twelve like-minded people who have enough time and interest to read selected materials
- One living room with sufficient comfortable seating
- One food & beverage item per member
- One volunteer timekeeper or discussion leader

Instructions:

1. Mix socially, stir intellectually, blend creatively and shape lovingly into a club designed for its members' interests.

2. Allow to gel for at least one cycle — usually a year — before judging its merits.

3. Repeat ... repeat ... repeat ...

---

across Canada. We hope that the recipes and suggestions contained in this book will help you to find or to establish a book club that is a rewarding and as eccentric as our own.

THE BOOK CLUB TRADITION

Book clubs are not a new phenomenon. Perhaps the earliest book clubs in Western society were Bible study groups, which have thrived continuously since the sixteenth century; debates centred around this fascinating collection of writings have at times led to religious schisms! Later on, the Chautauqua movement of the late nineteenth and early twentieth centuries provided a camp setting where folk debated books and issues in discussion groups.

Today, a tradition of communal discussion continues in settings such as the Elderhostel movement. The Book-of-the-Month Club is now more than seventy-five years old, and while it has changed over time, it gives every appearance of surviving for another three-quarters of a century and continuing to spawn profitable imitators. Book discussion forums and "chat groups" can be found on the World Wide Web as strangers meet electronically to exchange opinions on favourite authors, titles, themes and periods of literature.

Book clubs that take the form of a neighbourhood gathering or a group of friends who meet regularly with the express purpose of debating the merits of particular books have only appeared on the literary scene in significant numbers over the past two or three decades, and their popularity has increased enormously in recent years. Reasons for this rapid expansion of neighbourhood or work-related book clubs are obscure. It is evident that in recent years more reading is being done by the population at large. In addition, the well-documented baby-boomer population is now nearing retirement. Members of this demographically dominant group who are educated, opinionated, gregarious and have more time to read might well develop a desire to discuss what they read with like-minded people.

The book club phenomenon may also be a reaction to the isolation of modern, technologically oriented leisure activities involving computers and televisions. We all hunger for significant human interaction, and book clubs can provide a simple and satisfying method to develop friendships characterized by spirited debate.

OPTIONS FOR BOOK CLUBS

Whatever the explanation for the proliferation of book clubs, there are now sufficient numbers of successful clubs to offer a body of collective knowledge to those ready to embark on this adventure. While we don't see SWIVEL as the only book club model, our way of operating works well for us and might well provide ideas or guidelines to others interested in organizing a book club.

There are a wide variety of ways to organize a book club. Some clubs are loose collections of friends with an emphasis on socializing plus a little book talk thrown in during the evening. Other clubs are more formal, with detailed reading lists, specific tasks assigned to members and procedures that ensure that everyone has an equal opportunity to participate. Some clubs meet primarily for chat, and food is limited to beverages and dessert. Others are full-scale dinner parties with time reserved for book discussion.

CREATING A SCHEDULE

It is important to make sure that all members' interests are represented in the book list chosen for the year. At SWIVEL we draw up the book list for the following year at one of our last meetings of the current year — usually in the late spring or early summer. Each person makes one or two suggestions. Through discussion, as duplicates and topics of minor interest are eliminated, this "short list" is narrowed down to a program for the coming year. Once this is done, a schedule is set up and meeting dates chosen. To ensure both choice and structure, we have identified four types of readings:

- a single book;
- the works of a single author;
- a genre (for example, biography, mystery, travel);
- a subject or topic (for example, the pilgrimage to Santiago de Compostela).

These four types of readings are reflected in the four sections of this book.

THE ROLE OF THE HOST

Unlike the host of a dinner party, the book club hosts are not in control of the evening. They may be able to shepherd the group from one space to another, but beyond that, there's no being in charge. Indeed, their main functions are as butler or maid, social secretary (members unable to attend may contact the host), assigner of stove, microwave and oven space, and animal attendant. Hosts are kept busy greeting newcomers at the door, finding kitchen space for the various dishes, providing instructions for kitchen equipment and offering drinks before the members, starved from the day, seek out the appetizers.

After years of experience, we have found that as host, it is wise to have a few emergency items on hand. A loaf of good bread and something to spread on it or perhaps a selection of nuts and pretzels will be handy if the evening's menu turns out to have no appetizers. The bread can also be used to help out a rather thin main course. Frozen items that can be pulled out for an impromptu dessert are also useful.

The host's final job of the evening is retrieval. After an evening of enthusiastic discussion, guests may fly out the door leaving dishes or containers behind (or occasionally, taking someone else's). E-mail is excellent for following up on misplaced items.

ON SKIPPING

There will be times when members are unable to read the work chosen for the evening, or perhaps to contribute to the meal. Dealing with this is something individual clubs work out for themselves. At SWIVEL we tend to be rather gentle in dealing with "skippers."

Contributing to the meal, even for those who are frantically busy, needn't be a burden. Perfectly acceptable offerings — such as a loaf of bread, several pieces of cheese, a salad or two from the deli counter, or a selection of fresh fruit — can be obtained at a convenience store or supermarket on the way to the meeting. Probably the most inspired store-bought contribution we ever had was the box of chocolate cigars (which turned out to be the only dessert!) for an evening devoted to books on the Dionne quintuplets.

Skipping that involves reading — that is, not reading the selection at all, reading only part of it, or reading the wrong book — can be more problematic. In most clubs it is considered good form for individuals who for one reason or another have been unable to read the evening's selection to remain silent. However, if the club is a chatty group — as SWIVEL is — there will be some tolerance for off-topic digressions. Skipping is more acceptable if the person has been able to at least read part of the selection. She or he will have something to contribute to the discussion, and an explanation of the reason for not finishing the book, if the reason is literary, may be interesting in itself. Reading the wrong book, along with explanations of why and how the error was made, can often be the subject of much hilarity.

INVITATIONS

Although invitations may seem a frivolous indulgence, it is important to remember that book clubs typically appeal to busy people. If the group is larger than four or five members, a reminder of some sort prior to each meeting will be appreciated. Options range from telephone calls to mailed meeting announcements, e-mail reminders or full-scale invitations.

Probably one element of the glue that has kept SWIVEL together as a group through the years, is the ongoing series of wonderful invitations created by Bob. They summon us to enjoyable evenings of fun and intellectual activity with delectable dishes worthy of sharing. Often a second member takes responsibility for delivering these invitations, and one of our members has also been carefully collecting them in a small archive. These creative missives have served to remind us of not only the date and the readings but also the time and talent expended by our members in preparing for these evenings.

ON PARTNERS, CHILDREN AND PETS

Since book clubs generally meet in a member's home, one important question to be settled is the role of other occupants. As with other decisions involving meetings, each individual club can work out an arrangement that best suits individual members.

SWIVEL supports the Victorian maxim that children should be seen but not heard. Usually they are seen departing with a non-member spouse, but we are, of course, delighted to exchange a word of greeting as they leave. Their reward for this temporary banishment is a selection of excellent leftovers for the next day. The same rule — and reward — generally applies to partners, but we always invite them to share the meal with us and occasionally our invitation is accepted. Indeed, over the years we have benefited from several husband-wife teams as members.

Pets are generally less of a problem for club meetings. Indeed, at SWIVEL, with partners and children aside, we exercise full license to admire and romp with family pets, all of whom are eager to be both seen and heard.

ONE PARTNER'S VIEW

"From my basement study, I do not so much observe SWIVEL in operation as hear it. Peals of laughter frequently punctuate the enthusiastic discussion. These people clearly are having an animated and happy time. And the leftovers are wonderful!"

MODUS OPERANDI AND TRADITIONS

A book club can be a rather informal group, but most clubs find they need some structure in order to operate efficiently. Such a structure might involve procedures for the transition from the meal to the evening's discussion for determining the format of the discussion and for inviting new members to join the group. At SWIVEL, for example, new members are invited to join after consultation with the group as a whole.

The blissful pleasures of food can present a tangible distraction for a book club. With the heady mix of fine conversation, delicious victuals and complementary beverages, it is sometimes difficult to adjourn for the book discussion. At SWIVEL, we designate one of our number to remind us that book-talk time has arrived.

Some groups may enjoy a non-structured atmosphere, while others may choose, at least in the early part of the discussion, to speak in turn. At SWIVEL, we like an orderly discussion, with everyone around the circle giving their comments (or perhaps mumbling an excuse). Discussions involving literature can often become quite animated, but such altercations can, and should, remain civilized, with the opponents making a continual effort to listen to each other.

HAVING FUN

Don't just discuss books, sing them! One of the book selections we chose profiled hymns. This reminded several of the members of childhood experiences in Sunday School and choir, to say nothing of youth groups, church summer camps, and church services. As one member sang a few lines to recover the lyrics of a hymn, she was joined by one after another — lapsed church-goers all — who hummed, or sang in full-throated harmonies, the hymns of our youth. We were surprised at the pleasure of singing old hymns again and have tried to give ourselves licence to do so more often, sometimes in harmony with our dogs.

ONE MEMBER'S FIRST NIGHT JITTERS

"That first night was not unlike the first day of high school — something approaching fear or trepidation. What should I wear? Will I be on time? Will I know any other people? Will I fit in? My choice of book is probably all wrong! But off I went, probably overdressed and far too nervous about the humble casserole under my arm. I needn't have worried. It was clear from the beginning that this book club was a celebration — a celebration of good food, good drink, varied reading, high-energy debate, freedom to speak one's mind, and always, always laughter. I felt welcome at once, and the hostess knew my brother, for heaven's sake!

"I had been told that dinner would be potluck, but that night it was impossible to believe that it wasn't carefully planned: two appetizers, three salads, a perfectly roasted chicken, homemade bread, three desserts, red and white wine, tea and coffee. Not so, everyone assured me. Just serendipity.

"Funny, I can't remember what we read, but I do remember thinking on the way home how much I was looking forward to the next meeting in two months. For many of us, anticipation is the signature tune of our book club. No matter the stresses and strains of teaching or family life, or the odd twinge of middle age, a night at the book club seems to put things in perspective. A night to look forward to ... a grand night out."

THE INTREPID SURFER

Afraid of new technology? Unsure of what to do on the Internet? Have a look at Debbie Flanagan's wonderful Web site "Finding It Online: Web Search Strategies" at http://home.sprintmail.com/~debflanagan/main.html. Flanagan gives clear instructions for preparing a search. She suggests search strategies and offers lots of practice. There's a wealth of good information out there about books and authors — and cooking — just waiting to be found.

Section One

ORGANIZING
BOOK CLUB MEETINGS
BY SINGLE TITLE

Invitations for SWIVEL meetings

1/ ELECTRICITY

"No-Fail" Suggestions to Spark Discussion

APPETIZERS

Savoury Miniature Puffs

Cheese Torta with Pesto Sauce

Mushroom Turnovers

MAIN COURSES

Lamb Stuffed with Spinach,
Mint & Tomato*

Vegetarian Pilau

Chicken Curry

Tomato-Basil Tart

Basic Tossed Salad

DESSERTS

Easy Chocolate Cake

Lemon Curd

Sticky Toffee Puddings with Toffee Sauce

Apricot Squares

Chocolate Raisin Bread Pudding

* hostess choice

DISCUSSING A SINGLE WORK

When club members read different books on a given theme or topic, the evening is often characterized by active listening as individual members describe the books they have chosen. A book club evening based on a single work, however, will usually result in more active discussion and lively debate. Both formats work well — one is no better than the other — and a book club year will benefit by a healthy mix of the two. The level of active participation in discussions of a single work is not surprising, since everyone shares a common focus. Although members of a club may well share a common bond (for example, the members of SWIVEL are all teachers), individuals bring their own life stories, travel experiences and subject specialties to the table. A historian might enlighten a psychology major on the process of cause and effect. A specialist in English may extend the metaphor of interpretation well beyond the patience of a scientist.

A SPIRITED DISCUSSION

At SWIVEL, we agree, we disagree and we question, all in a spirit of friendship. We attack and defend book characters as if they were real people — perhaps even relatives. Most members bring a copy of the book to the meeting. Often points are made by reading a short passage to support an argument, waving the book in the air or emphatically thumping the cover. At our discussion of Victoria Glendinning's *Electricity,* there was a sea of blue-black covers on laps, on tables and under chairs, most with book-marked passages. Although our timekeeper is responsible for signalling the formal start of our discussions, small pockets of conversation often start over nibblies in the kitchen. Often the trigger is a simple question such as, "Did you like it?" If the evening has been particularly spirited, we might still be winding down the exchange as we pack up our dishes and put on our coats.

PREPARING FOR DISCUSSION

For new members of established clubs, there may be apprehension about the type or level of discussion that can take place. For new book clubs, there may be similar worries about how to begin a discussion or how to keep it focused while not too regimented. Questions may be helpful, especially at the beginning, but the choice of book makes a difference too. The sidebars throughout this chapter offer examples of books that are almost guaranteed to provoke discussion and debate.

One cannot think well, love well, sleep well, unless one has dined well.

VIRGINIA WOOLF,
*A ROOM OF
ONE'S OWN,
1929*

Savoury Miniature Puffs

These tasty morsels offer multiple possibilities. If you want to avoid meat, add a little mayonnaise to some cream cheese and mix in finely chopped onion and cucumber or perhaps ripe olives.

1/2 cup	water	125 mL
1/4 cup	butter or margarine	50 mL
1/8 tsp	salt	.5 mL
1/2 cup	flour	125 mL
1/4 cup	finely grated Cheddar cheese (optional)	50 mL
2 eggs		
1 1/2 cup	chopped ham, chicken, shrimp or crab	375 mL
2 tbsp	minced celery or water chestnuts	25 mL
1 tsp	minced onion	5 mL
3–4 tbsp	mayonnaise	45–60 mL
salt (to taste)		

1. Preheat oven to 400°F (200°C).
2. Combine water and butter in a saucepan; bring to a boil. Add salt and flour all at once and stir quickly until the mixture forms a ball. Remove from heat. Add cheese, if desired.
3. Add eggs, one at a time, and beat well until the mixture is like velvet.
4. Refrigerate mixture for one hour.
5. Place teaspoonsful of batter on a lightly greased cookie sheet.
6. Bake for 15 to 18 minutes or until the puffs are golden brown.
7. Combine meat or seafood, celery, onion, mayonnaise and salt, and mix well.
8. When puffs have cooled slightly, cut in half and fill.

Makes 4 to 5 dozen puffs.

Cheese Torta

Keep clear of the devouring mob when you serve this deservedly popular appetizer! Adjust the garlic to your taste, and feel free to use more pesto. Serve with slices of baguette.

6 oz	goat cheese	170 g
4 oz	cream cheese	125 g
2–8 cloves garlic, peeled and crushed		
salt and pepper (to taste)		
1/2 cup	Pesto Sauce (recipe follows)	125 mL
1/2 cup	oil-packed sun-dried tomatoes, finely chopped,	
	plus 1–2 tsp (5–10 mL) of the marinade oil	125 mL
fresh herbs (sprigs of thyme, oregano, rosemary, parsley)		
for garnish		

1. Combine goat cheese and cream cheese, then add the garlic. Add salt and black pepper to taste.

2. Line a small glass bowl (about 2–3 cups / 500–750 mL) with plastic wrap. Place one third of the cheese mixture in the bowl. Top with Pesto Sauce. Put another third of the cheese on top of this, and add the sun-dried tomatoes. Top with the remaining cheese.

3. Cover with plastic wrap and chill for at least 2 hours, or up to four days.

4. To serve, invert bowl on a serving dish. Remove plastic wrap and garnish with sprigs of fresh herbs.

Serves 20 to 25 with other hors d'oeuvres.

Charles Frazier's novel COLD MOUNTAIN *(1997) is a National Book Award winner. In the last months of the American Civil War, Inman, a wounded Confederate veteran, begins the long journey back to his home in the hills of North Carolina. As Inman travels home to his love, Ada, he meets rogues and outlaws. Ada, who does not stray far from home, encounters unique people who accompany her on a journey of self-knowledge.*

Pesto Sauce

2 cloves	garlic	
1 tsp	salt	5 mL
3 cups	fresh basil leaves, packed	750 mL
2 tbsp	pine nuts	25 mL
2 tbsp	fresh parsley, chopped (optional)	25 mL
1/2 cup	olive oil	125 mL
1/2 cup	finely grated fresh Parmesan cheese	125 mL

1. Place all ingredients except cheese in a processor or blender.
2. Blend until mixture is thoroughly puréed. Beat in the cheese.

Makes about 1 cup (250 mL).

On the surface, The POISONWOOD BIBLE (1998) by Barbara Kingsolver is a fascinating portrayal of an American wife and four daughters who are very nearly destroyed by the obsessed patriarch of the family. To read this novel is to begin to understand the legacy of European colonialism and the bloody interference of the American government in the affairs of the Congo. Kingsolver convincingly challenges the perception of "civilized" nations helping to develop the African continent.

Mushroom Turnovers

To vary the flavour, substitute any herb of your choice for the thyme.

9 oz	cream cheese	270 g
1 cup	butter or margarine	250 mL
2 cups	all-purpose flour	500 mL
8 oz	mushrooms, minced	250 g
1/2	onion, minced	
3 tbsp	butter	45 mL
2 tbsp	all-purpose flour	25 mL
1/4 tsp	salt	1 mL
1/2 tsp	thyme	2 mL
1/4 tsp	pepper	1 mL
1 tbsp	dry sherry	15 mL
1/4 cup	sour cream	50 mL
1	egg yolk	
1 tbsp	water	15 mL

1. Preheat oven to 375°F (190°C).
2. Cream together cheese and butter. Add flour and form into a dough. Divide into three balls. Wrap each in waxed paper and chill at least 1 hour.
3. Sauté mushrooms and onion in butter until soft. Stir in flour, salt, thyme, pepper and sherry. Cook until well blended. Remove from heat. Stir in sour cream and allow mixture to cool.
4. Roll dough to 1/8-inch (3-mm) thickness on a lightly floured board. Cut out 3-inch (8-cm) circles. Place 1 tbsp (15 mL) filling on each circle and fold in half, stretching the dough and crimping the edges with a fork.
5. Combine egg yolk and water to make an egg wash and brush over each turnover.
6. Bake for 15 to 20 minutes or until golden brown.

Makes 35 to 40 turnovers.

In A FINE BALANCE (1995), Rohinton Mistry traces the lives of four characters in the India of the 1970s. The reader is introduced to the rigid discrimination of the caste system and, while Mistry describes much cruelty and suffering, he also illuminates the lives of the poor, demonstrating a love of family, a spirit of goodness and a never-ending hope even in the face of overwhelming political and social evil. Mistry's characters are unforgettable; he makes the reader see and understand the nature of the society that sustains them.

Lamb Stuffed with Spinach, Mint and Tomato

THE PEPPERED MOTH

(2001) by Margaret Drabble is a semi-autobiographical novel in which Drabble seeks to come to terms with memories of her mother, whom she describes as "highly intelligent, angry and deeply disappointed." More than a personal account, the novel is a social history about a generation of women whose lives were blighted by their acceptance of a system in which their talents could only be used in prescribed ways.

This colourful and festive entrée will provide a marvellous centrepiece for any potluck.

1/4 cup	butter	50 mL
1 small clove garlic, minced		
1 1/2 cups	soft bread crumbs	375 mL
12 oz pkg.	frozen spinach, thawed and squeezed dry	375 mL
1/2 cup	chopped fresh mint	125 mL
3 tbsp	mint sauce	45 mL
1/2 tsp	salt	2 mL
1/4 tsp	pepper	1 mL
5 lb leg of lamb, boned	2.5 kg	
1 tbsp	butter	15 mL
2 tomatoes peeled, seeded and chopped		
dry mustard (to taste)		
crushed garlic (to taste)		
freshly ground black pepper (to taste)		
2 tbsp	all-purpose flour	25 mL
2 cups	stock or water	500 mL

1. Preheat oven to 325°F (160°C).
2. To make spinach stuffing, heat butter in a skillet. Add garlic and sauté. Add bread crumbs and cook until lightly browned. Add spinach and toss with crumbs for 1 minute. Remove from heat;

add mint, mint sauce, salt and pepper. Toss together.

3. Lay lamb out flat. Spread evenly with spinach mixture.

4. Melt 1 tablespoon butter in the skillet. Add tomatoes and cook gently until just hot. Spread over spinach.

5. Roll lamb around stuffing and tie securely. Combine dry mustard, garlic and pepper and rub over outside of roast. Place lamb in a shallow roasting pan. Roast uncovered for approximately 2 hours or until a meat thermometer registers 160°F (60°C) for medium.

Serves 6 to 8.

It is difficult to think anything but pleasant thoughts while eating a homegrown tomato.

LEWIS GRIZZARD

Vegetarian Pilau

This rice dish is mildly spiced and full of vegetables. It can be made up to two days ahead, but be careful to reheat it gently.

1/4 cup	butter	50 mL
2 medium onions, sliced		
1 cup	raw cauliflower florets	250 mL
1 cup	raw finely diced potato	250 mL
2 small yellow zucchini, sliced		
1 cup	sliced carrots	250 mL
1 medium sweet red pepper, diced		
1/2 tsp	ground turmeric	2 mL
1/2 tsp	ground ginger	2 mL
1 tsp	curry powder	5 mL
1 tsp	ground cumin	5 mL
1 bay leaf		
4 cloves		
1–1 1/2 tsp cracked black pepper		5–7 mL
1 1/2 cups	long grain white rice	375 mL
4 cups	boiling water or vegetable stock	1 L
1 cup	frozen green peas	250 mL
1 cup	currants	250 mL
1/2 cup	slivered almonds	125 mL
fresh coriander (optional, for garnish)		

1. Preheat oven to 300°F (150°C).
2. Melt butter in a large deep frying pan. Add onions and cook until golden. Remove from pan and set aside.

3. Add cauliflower, potato, zucchini and carrots to pan and sauté until tender. Add red pepper during the last 2 minutes of cooking. Remove from pan, combine with onions and set aside.

4. Place turmeric, ginger, curry powder, cumin, bay leaf, cloves and pepper in pan. Cook on high for 1 minute, stirring constantly. Add rice and fry for 2 minutes, stirring constantly.

5. Add boiling water or vegetable stock to the rice and spice mixture and continue boiling until the water is almost gone.

6. Remove from heat. Stir in onion mixture, frozen peas and currants.

7. Pour into a casserole dish. Cover and bake for 15 to 20 minutes.

8. Before serving, sprinkle almonds on top and garnish with fresh coriander if desired.

Serves 6.

Our lives are not in the lap of the gods, but in the lap of our cooks.

LIN YUTANG,
THE IMPORTANCE
OF LIVING,
1937

Chicken Curry

Chicken and curry is a favourite combination.
This easy casserole can be made the day before.

1 1/2 lb	chicken breast, skinned and boned	750 g
1/2 lb	potatoes, peeled	250 g
2 tbsp	vegetable oil	25 mL
1 tbsp	red curry paste	15 mL
1 tbsp	curry powder	15 mL
16 oz can	coconut milk	400 mL
3 tbsp	granulated sugar	45 mL
3 tbsp	fish sauce	45 mL

1. Cut chicken and potatoes into 1-inch (2.5-cm) cubes.

2. In a wok or frying pan, heat oil until hot. Add curry paste and curry powder. Reduce heat to medium and stir-fry the spice mixture for 2 minutes.

3. Add coconut milk to the pan, stirring to mix well. Add the chicken and cook for 10 minutes. Add the potatoes and cook until tender, about 20 minutes. Flavour the curry with sugar and fish sauce, stirring until the sugar has melted and the flavours have melded.

4. If carrying to a potluck, transport in a casserole dish. Reheat, covered, for about 10 minutes at 325°F (160°C).

Serves 6.

Tomato-Basil Tart

This savoury tart is pleasantly summery and can be especially refreshing on a hot day, served either chilled or at room temperature.

1 9-inch (23-cm) unbaked pie shell		
3 tbsp	butter	45 mL
2 cooking onions, finely chopped		
2 lbs	fresh tomatoes, peeled, seeded and chopped	1 kg
1 cup	whipping cream	250 mL
3 eggs		
1 1/2 tsp	salt	7 mL
1/2 tsp	freshly ground pepper	2 mL
3 tbsp	chopped fresh basil	45 mL
2 tsp	finely minced green onions	25 mL

1. Preheat oven to 350°F (180°C).
2. Bake pie shell for 10 minutes. Remove from oven and set aside.
3. Melt butter in a frying pan, add onions and sauté until transparent.
4. Strain chopped tomatoes through a sieve and add to onions. Cook over low heat until partially thickened. Remove from heat.
5. Beat together cream and eggs and add to tomato mixture. Season with salt and pepper. Stir in basil and green onions. Pour mixture into pie shell.
6. Bake tart for 30 to 35 minutes or until a knife inserted in the centre comes out clean. Let set for 10 minutes.

Serves 6 to 8.

꙳

FUGITIVE PIECES *(1996) by Anne Michaels is a riveting study of the transformative effects of war on two men from different generations. In many ways, it is two separate, though linked, novels. The story is set in Greece, Poland and Toronto, but the characters view themselves as outsiders to their societies. The novel is a study in forms as well as a compelling story, and is as much poetry as narrative.*

꙳

Basic Tossed Salad

A tossed salad can serve as a basis for personal invention. Try any of the additions listed below, or create your own special dish. You can substitute commercially packaged salad greens, or your own choice of three or four different varieties of greens. Salad greens should be washed and shaken or whirled dry, wrapped in paper towels, placed in a plastic bag and refrigerated until needed.

BASIC SALAD

4 cups	mesclun mix or salad greens	1 L
1 red onion, thinly sliced (or to taste)		

BASIC VINAIGRETTE

1 tbsp	lemon juice or vinegar 15 mL
3–4 tbsp	olive oil 45–60 mL
1 tsp	Dijon mustard (or to taste) 5 mL
pinch sea salt	

ADDITIONS

- pieces of cooked fresh asparagus and crumbled Roquefort, feta or sharp Cheddar cheese
- avocado chunks, large pieces of orange segments, slivered red pepper and feta cheese
- avocado chunks, large pieces of diced cucumber, sliced radishes and blue cheese
- artichoke hearts or hearts of palm, slivered green, red or yellow peppers and crumbled Roquefort cheese

---

In CLARA CALLAN (2001), Richard B. Wright tells the story of two sisters who struggle with what is expected of them and what they desire out of life. Set in the late 1930s, everyday experiences are shared through Clara's journal entries and through letters exchanged between the sisters. Clara's struggle takes place in a rural community of Ontario where she is a teacher, whereas Nora's takes place in New York amid the world of radio soaps. The Giller Prize jury described this novel as an "intimate glimpse into the psyches of two different yet inextricably connected women."

- cooked shrimp, capers and strips of pink grapefruit
- chunks of fresh mango, red pepper slices, cashews and 1-lb shrimp (with or without tails) that have been marinated for 1 to 4 hours in the refrigerator in a marinade of 1 tsp (5 mL) olive oil, 1 tbsp (15 mL) finely chopped fresh ginger, the juice of one lime, one crushed clove of garlic, 1/4 tsp (1 mL) red pepper flakes and 1/4 cup (50 mL) chopped coriander.

Use additional marinade instead of the regular vinaigrette to dress the salad.
(Caution: Do not reuse marinade that has been used to marinate the shrimp.)

1. Wash salad greens, dry and wrap in paper towels.
2. Prepare additional ingredients of choice.
3. Combine vinaigrette ingredients in a jar and shake well to blend.
4. Keep all ingredients cool until serving time. To serve, combine salad ingredients in large salad bowl and dress lightly with vinaigrette.

Serves 4.

A cucumber should be well sliced and dressed with pepper and vinegar, and then thrown out as good for nothing.

SAMUEL JOHNSON
QUOTED IN JAMES BOSWELL,
TOUR OF THE HEBRIDES,
1785

Easy Chocolate Cake

Arthur Golden's MEMOIRS OF A GEISHA *(1997) is a compelling and sympathetic look at the secretive and mysterious world of the geisha. Recounted as the dictated memoirs of Chiyo, a young Japanese girl who is sold by her family, the novel paints an exquisitely detailed picture of the customs and rituals of geisha society. Chiyo becomes a highly renowned geisha but struggles to retain some independence within this slavelike social structure where women are trained to beguile powerful men. The novel raises as many questions as it answers.*

Serve this tasty gâteau with seasonal fresh fruit and vanilla frozen yogurt.

2 cups	sifted cake flour	500 mL
1 1/2 cups	granulated sugar	375 mL
3/4 cup	sifted cocoa	175 mL
1 1/2 tsp	baking powder	7 mL
1/2 tsp	baking soda	2 mL
1 tsp	salt	2 mL
1/2 cup	very soft butter	125 mL
2 eggs		
1 1/2 cups	buttermilk	375 mL
1 tsp	vanilla	5 mL
1/2 cup	hot water	125 mL

1. Preheat oven to 350°F (180°C).
2. Put all ingredients except hot water in a large mixing bowl and beat at low speed for 1 minute. Increase beater speed to medium and beat for 2 more minutes. Add hot water and mix lightly.
3. Pour batter into a non-stick 8-inch (2.5-L) square cake pan.
4. Bake for 30 minutes.

Serves 12 to 14.

Lemon Curd

Pam Collacott has updated this ever-reliable recipe for the microwave in her wonderful book THE BEST OF NEW WAVE COOKING. *At serving time, spoon the curd into baked tart shells and top with whipped cream. Another option is to top the curd tarts with meringue (see recipe p. 132) and brown them briefly under the broiler.*

2 large eggs		
1 cup	granulated sugar	250 mL
2 tbsp	grated lemon zest	25 mL
3 tbsp	butter	45 mL
1/2 cup	fresh lemon juice	125 mL

1. Whisk eggs and sugar together until smooth. Whisk in lemon juice and stir in butter and grated zest.
2. Microwave on high for about 4 minutes, whisking once every minute, until mixture boils and thickens.
3. Cool and store in the refrigerator.

Makes 1 1/2 cups (375 mL).

Wayson Choy's THE JADE PEONY *(1995) was a co-winner of the 1995 Trillium Award for best book. In this novel, life in Vancouver's Chinatown is viewed from the perspective of the three youngest children of an immigrant family. Set against the economic hardship and racial prejudice of the 1930s and 1940s, each child's experiences of those years are coloured by family birth position, gender and above all the influence of Poh-Poh, their grandmother, who keeps the culture of Old China alive in the history of her pieces of beautiful jade.*

Sticky Toffee Puddings with Toffee Sauce

*These simple sweet puddings offer warm comfort on a cold winter's night.
Serve them with whipped cream or ice cream. The sauce can be easily
made in the microwave.*

TOFFEE SAUCE

1 cup	golden brown sugar, packed	250 mL
2/3 cup	butter	150 mL
1/2 cup	whipping cream	125 mL

Combine sugar, butter and cream in a medium saucepan. Cook over
medium-high heat, stirring occasionally, for about 5 minutes or
until sugar and butter have melted and sauce is bubbly. Remove
from heat and set aside.

Makes 1 1/2 cups.

TOFFEE PUDDING

3/4 cup	sultana raisins	175 mL
3/4 cup	boiling water	175 mL
1 1/4 cup	all-purpose flour	300 mL
1 tsp	baking powder	5 mL
1/4 tsp	salt	1 mL
1/2 cup	golden brown sugar, packed	125 mL
1/3 cup	butter, softened	75 mL
2 eggs		
1 tsp	vanilla	5 mL

1. Preheat the oven to 350°F (180°C). Butter eight 3/4-cup (175-mL) custard cups and arrange on a baking sheet.

2. In a small heat-proof bowl, soak raisins in boiling water for 15 minutes. Drain, reserving liquid and raisins separately.

3. In a medium bowl, stir together flour, baking powder and salt.

4. In a separate bowl, beat together sugar and butter until fluffy. Beat in eggs one at a time, and then beat in vanilla. Fold flour into sugar mixture alternately with liquid from raisins. Fold in raisins.

5. Spoon 1 tbsp (15 mL) Toffee Sauce into each custard cup. Spoon about 1/3 cup (75 mL) Toffee Pudding into each custard cup. Bake for 20 to 25 minutes, until light golden and firm. Remove from oven and let stand for 5 minutes.

6. Meanwhile, reheat remaining Toffee Sauce until bubbly. To serve, run a knife around sides of each custard cup and unmould the puddings onto plates. Drizzle Toffee Sauce over each pudding.

Serves 8.

The hostess must be like the duck — calm and unruffled on the surface, and paddling like hell underneath.

ANONYMOUS

Apricot Squares

These tasty treats are interesting and different.

FILLING

2/3 cup	dried apricots	150 mL
1 cup	water	250 mL
2 egg yolks		
3/4 cup	brown sugar, packed	175 mL
1/2 cup	all-purpose flour	125 mL
1/2 tsp	baking powder	2 mL
1/4 tsp	salt	1 mL

BASE

1/2 cup	butter, softened	125 mL
1 cup	all-purpose flour	250 mL
1/4 cup	granulated sugar	50 mL

ICING

1 3/4 cups icing sugar		425 mL
1/4 cup	butter, softened	50 mL
1 tbsp	lemon juice	15 mL
1 1/2 tsp	grated lemon zest	7 mL

1. Preheat oven to 325°F (160°C).

2. To make the filling, cut apricots into small pieces. In a heavy saucepan, combine apricots with water and bring to a boil; simmer, uncovered, for about 20 minutes or until most of

the water is absorbed and apricots are tender. Set aside.

3. Meanwhile, make the base. In a bowl, cream butter. Add flour and sugar and mix well. Press into the bottom of an 8-inch (2.5-L) square cake pan and bake for about 20 minutes or until golden. Set aside.

4. Continue with filling. In a bowl, beat egg yolks with an electric mixer for 1 minute. Add brown sugar and beat 1 minute. Stir in flour, baking powder and salt and mix well. Blend in apricot mixture. Spread filling over the warm base.

5. Bake for 30 to 40 minutes or until top is golden and springs back when lightly touched. Cool.

6. Combine ingredients for icing in a small bowl and mix until smooth. Spread over the cooled apricot filling — be careful, as it is fragile. Cut into small squares to serve.

Makes 12 to 16 squares.

A practical cookbook is one that has a blank page in the back — where you list the numbers of the nearest delicatessen.

ANONYMOUS

Chocolate Raisin Bread Pudding

This dessert represents a delightful transformation of a crust of bread.

4 large eggs		
1 cup	whole milk	250 mL
1 cup	35% cream	250 mL
1 cup	10% cream	250 mL
1 cup	granulated sugar	250 mL
1/4 cup	sifted unsweetened cocoa powder	50 mL
1 tbsp	vanilla extract	15 mL
1/2 tsp	salt	2 mL
8 cups	1-inch (2.5-cm) bread cubes	2L
	(cut from an unsliced crusty loaf)	
1/2 cup	semisweet chocolate chips	125 mL
1/2 cup	golden raisins	125 mL

1. Preheat oven to 350°F (180°C). Butter a 9x13-inch (3.5-L) baking pan.

2. In a large bowl, whisk together eggs, milk, creams, sugar, cocoa, vanilla and salt.

3. Add bread and stir until cubes are coated. Let stand 5 minutes. Stir in chocolate chips and raisins. Transfer pudding to baking pan.

4. Bake in a hot water bath in middle of oven until pudding is just set, about 40 minutes. Serve warm.

Serves 6 to 8.

2/ FALL ON YOUR KNEES

CHARACTERS IN FOCUS

APPETIZERS

Yogurt Cheese Dip

Orange Hummus

Marinated Goat Cheese Appetizer

MAIN COURSES

Curried Lamb

Spanokopita

Irene's Tabouleh

Baked Beans

Eggplant Casserole

DESSERTS

Maritime Blueberry Pudding

Oatmeal Cookies

Baklava

Johnny Cake

SHARPENING THE DISCUSSION

While it may be true that some writers concentrate first on the situation when writing fiction, it is without question the characters that dominate book club discussions.

When you listen to radio or television programs about books or detach yourself sufficiently to eavesdrop on your own club's discussions, you are bound to hear lively and often heated debate about fictional characters. Sometimes the focus is on their connections with each other, for example, through family bonds. Other times it is on their connections with the wider world or their historical context. More often than not, though, what brings these characters to the forefront of debate is how we see them reflected in our own context. We speculate on their motives and judge their degrees of wickedness or compassion as though they were real people. We defend their appeal to us when others find them unattractive. A simple declaration such as "He has some redeeming features" can send the noise level in the room soaring. On the night we discussed Ann-Marie MacDonald's *Fall On Your Knees,* we agreed on the merits and weaknesses of the female characters — even minor ones, such as Frances who sacrificed herself for the well-being of others. We could not, however, agree on the character of James, the father. Just how wicked was he? Some found sympathy for him while others could not.

The sidebars in this chapter introduce fictional characters that we might like to invite to dinner. (Perhaps not all to the *same* dinner, as the mix of the eccentric, the bizarre and the just plain interesting might defy compatibility.)

THE INTREPID SURFER

If you are looking for biographical information on living Canadian authors, the Web site of the National Library of Canada (www.nlc-bnc.ca) is a good place to start. The National Library site also provides links to organizations such as the Writers' Union of Canada and the Playwrights Union of Canada.

Yogurt Cheese Dip

This simple dip can serve as a base for a variety of flavouring choices. Serve it in a small bowl on a platter, surrounded with crudités, chips or crackers. If necessary you can substitute 1/4 tsp (1 mL) dried herbs for fresh herbs. This recipe transforms yogurt into a form of cheese that will keep for four or five days in the refrigerator.

3 cups	unflavoured low-fat yogurt	750 mL
1 tbsp	chopped fresh parsley	15 mL
1 tbsp	chopped chives or green onion	15 mL
1 tbsp	chopped fresh tarragon or dill	15 mL
2 garlic cloves, minced or crushed		
1 tsp	olive oil	5 mL
1/2 tsp	mild vinegar	2 mL
salt and pepper (to taste)		

1. Line a strainer with cheesecloth, paper towels or a coffee filter and place in a deep bowl. (The bottom of the strainer should not touch the liquid.)

2. Place yogurt in strainer set over a bowl to catch liquid. Cover with plastic wrap and refrigerate overnight.

3. When ready to use, transfer the yogurt in the strainer into a clean bowl. (Discard the liquid.) Add your choice of chives or onions, parsley, tarragon or dill with the garlic, oil and vinegar. Add salt and pepper and mix well.

Makes about 1 cup (250 mL).

Jane Urquhart,
THE STONE CARVERS
(2001)

I want to attend a dinner party given by Tilman, sit next to him (so he can't escape) and invite him to explain himself. Why did he regularly run away from home and family? Why the long silences, even from Klara, who had freed him from his shackles? Eventually, Tilman became a noted carver. With his heightened sense of shape and form, I'd like to see how his dinner table would be set. Since Tilman finally found happiness in opening his own restaurant, I would look forward to sampling his food, admiring his presentation and discussing his recipes.

Orange Hummus

This recipe is a pleasant variation of a famous Arabic dish. Serve it as an appetizer with pita bread. If you use canned chickpeas (rather than cooking your own), omit the salt. A food processor works well for mashing chickpeas.

2 cups	cooked chickpeas	500 mL
	(or 1 19-oz / 540-mL can, drained and rinsed)	
1/2 tsp	ground cumin	2 mL
1/4 tsp	ground coriander	1 mL
1/4 tsp	ground ginger	1 mL
1/2 tsp	dry mustard	2 mL
1/4 tsp	turmeric	1 mL
1/4 tsp	paprika	1 mL
3 tbsp	orange juice	45 mL
2 tbsp	tahini	25 mL
1 1/2 tsp	salt (omit with canned peas)	7 mL
1–2 tbsp	cider vinegar	15–25 mL
2 medium garlic cloves, crushed		
2 scallions, finely-minced (white and green)		
1–2 tsp	tamari sauce	5–10 mL

Mash the chickpeas and mix with the remaining ingredients. Cover and chill for at least 2 hours.

Makes about 3 cups (750 mL).

Marinated Goat Cheese Appetizer

Serve this delicate marriage of goat cheese and sun-dried tomatoes on a baguette. Begin preparation the day before to allow the cheese to marinate for a full twenty-four hours. This recipe features fresh rosemary, one of the most versatile of herbs. A little chopped rosemary will transform fresh orange sections and dumplings or biscuits. It is wonderful with lamb and pork, and has few equals for poultry stuffing.

6 oz	goat cheese	170 g
light olive oil (enough to cover goat cheese)		
1 1/2 oz	sun-dried tomatoes, drained and finely chopped	45 g
1/2 cup	pitted black olives	125 mL
1 large garlic clove, crushed		
1/4 cup	freshly chopped green onion	50 mL
2 tsp	finely chopped fresh rosemary	10 mL
1 fresh baguette		

1. Use a plastic thread to cut goat cheese into tiny cubes. Place in a shallow serving dish and cover with olive oil. (Too little oil will make the spread dry.) Add tomatoes, olives, garlic, onion and rosemary.

2. Marinate for 24 hours in the refrigerator.

3. To serve, cut baguette into thin slices and spread with marinated cheese.

Serves 8 to 10.

Bill Richardson,
BACHELOR BROTHERS
BED AND BREAKFAST
(1993)

Could we throw another potato in the pot and pull up two more chairs? I would like to invite Hector and Virgil, the proprietors of Bachelor Brothers Bed and Breakfast. Who knows, Hector might bring a casserole, Virgil might be tempted to play his bassoon, and both could suggest titles for our club from their lists "for the bath," "when feeling low," or other such occasions.

Curried Lamb

Here is a wonderful use for leftover cooked lamb. Applesauce replaces the traditional mango chutney for a distinctively Canadian twist. Serve it over hot fluffy rice. If desired, the curry can be accompanied by a variety of condiments — for example, chopped peanuts, banana slices, chopped hard-boiled egg, crumbled crisp bacon, chopped green onions or chives, chutney, raisins or shredded coconut — served in separate small dishes.

The word "curry" derives from the Hindustani word tucarri, which was colloquially shortened to turri and mispronounced by the English as "curry." Curry powder is actually a blend of many spices, usually including turmeric, cardamom, coriander, mustard, saffron and allspice.

3 slices bacon		
1/2 cup	sliced celery	125 mL
1 medium onion, finely chopped		
2 tbsp	all-purpose flour	25 mL
1 tbsp	curry powder	15 mL
3/4 tsp	salt	4 mL
1/2 tsp	turmeric	2 mL
1/2 cup	water	125 mL
1 cup	milk	250 mL
2 chicken bouillon cubes		
3/4 cup	sweetened applesauce	175 mL
2 tsp	granulated sugar	10 mL
2 tsp	lemon juice	10 mL
2 cups	cubed cooked lamb	500 mL

1. Fry bacon until crisp and cut into small pieces. Combine with celery and onion, stir and cook over medium heat for 5 minutes.

2. Remove bacon mixture from heat. Blend in flour, curry powder, salt and turmeric.

3. Stir in water and milk and add chicken bouillon cubes. Cook, stirring constantly, until thickened.

4. Stir in applesauce, sugar, lemon juice and lamb. Cover and simmer for 10 minutes, stirring occasionally.

5. If carrying as a potluck dish, both the curry and the rice can be refrigerated and then reheated before serving.

Serves about 4 as a main course.

At a dinner party, one should eat wisely but not too well, and talk well but not too wisely.

W. SOMERSET MAUGHAM,
A WRITER'S NOTEBOOK,
1896

Spanokopita

This spinach pie made with phyllo pastry captures the essence of the Mediterranean. It can be served hot or at room temperature, but do not reheat the pastry.

1/2 cup	olive oil	125 mL
2 cups	minced onion	500 mL
1/2 tsp	salt	2 mL
1/2 tsp	basil	2 mL
1/2 tsp	oregano	2 mL
10 oz	fresh spinach, washed and finely chopped	284 g
	(or 2 pkg)	
5 cloves garlic, minced		
3 tbsp	all-purpose flour	45 mL
3 cups	crumbled feta cheese	750 mL
1 cup	cottage cheese	250 mL
1 lb	pkg phyllo dough (about 20 sheets)	454 g

1. Preheat oven to 375°F (190°C). Lightly grease a 9 x 13-inch (3.5-L) baking pan.

2. Heat 1 tbsp (15 mL) of the olive oil in a Dutch oven or a large pot. (Reserve the rest of the oil for brushing the phyllo.) Add onions, salt, basil and oregano. Sauté for 5 minutes.

3. Add spinach. Turn up heat and cook rapidly until spinach is soft and wilted, about 5 to 8 minutes.

4. Stir in garlic. Sprinkle flour over the spinach, onion and garlic mixture, and cook over medium heat for 2 to 3 minutes.

5. Add crumbled feta cheese and cottage cheese. Taste and add additional seasonings if desired.

Margaret Atwood,
THE BLIND ASSASSIN
(2000)

What would Reenie bring to the table? An appreciation for both a simple loaf of bread and a twelve-course dinner. She would monitor who ate what. She might gossip a little. She would attribute to people the histories she felt they ought to have, or make comments such as, "He is not from the same pea patch as the rest of us." As the Chase's main-stay and protector of two little girls, Reenie earns a place at a fine table, if for no other reason, for the many times she said, "Tell me where it hurts."

6. Place one sheet of phyllo in baking pan so that it extends up the sides of the pan. Brush with oil. Place another sheet of phyllo in the opposite direction in the pan and brush with oil. Add 6 more sheets, alternating the direction and brushing each sheet with oil. Spread half the spinach filling evenly over the phyllo.

7. Add 8 more sheets of phyllo, using the same method as above. Spread with remaining spinach mixture and cover with remaining sheets of phyllo, alternating and brushing as before. Trim the edges and tuck in. Brush with oil.

8. Bake uncovered for 45 to 50 minutes or until brown and crisp.

Serves 8 to 10.

Mediterranean cooking... is lusty joyful food and it must be entered into in that spirit.

BYRON AYANOGLU,
SIMPLY MEDITERRANEAN
COOKING,
1998.

Irene's Tabouleh

Parsley, the jewel of herbs, is said to signify both revelry and victory. Garlands of parsley were used to crown champions of the Olympic Games in ancient Greece.

1 1/2 cups	water	375 ml
1 cup	bulgar	250 mL
1 1/2 tsp	salt	7 mL
1/3 cup	fresh lemon juice	75 ml
1/2–1 tsp	minced garlic	2–5 mL
1/2 cup	chopped green onion	125 mL
1 1/2 tsp	minced fresh mint	7 mL
1/4 cup	olive oil	50 mL
1 cup	minced fresh parsley	250 mL

OPTIONAL INGREDIENTS

1/2 cup each	chopped ripe tomatoes,	125 mL
	chopped English cucumber, grated carrot,	
	green pepper, chickpeas or radish	

1. Boil water and pour over bulgar and salt. Let stand 20 minutes or until bulgar has softened and all the water is absorbed. Pat dry.
2. Add lemon juice, garlic, onion, mint, oil and parsley. Mix well. Refrigerate for 2 to 3 hours to blend flavours.
3. Just before serving, add optional ingredients as desired and mix well.

Serves 6 to 8.

Katherine Govier,
ANGEL WALK
(1996)

Cory Ditchburn, a war correspondent and photographer during the Second World War, is the subject of a retrospective arranged by her son. The photographs, Govier tells us, are a true story, but they do not represent the only possible story of Ditchburn's life. It would be fascinating to invite her to dinner — in her signature pencil-thin black pants, antique lace blouse and black blazer — to tell us the other stories, the ones that illuminate the alternative meanings of the celebrated photographs.

Baked Beans

Fool them all with this quicker, easier version of baked beans!

28 oz	pork and beans (2 cans)	796 mL
1 medium onion, diced		
2 tsp	prepared mustard	10 mL
1/4 cup	ketchup	50 mL
1/4 cup	barbeque sauce	50 mL
1/4 cup	molasses	50 mL
1/3 cup	brown sugar	75 mL

Combine all ingredients in an ovenproof casserole. Cover and
bake for 3 to 4 hours at 300°F (150°C). Uncover for the
last half hour so the beans will brown a little.

Serves 4 to 6.

Wayne Johnson,
THE COLONY OF
UNREQUITED DREAMS
(1998)

Sheilagh Fielding "was the sort of woman people called by her last name," who, silver flask in hand, stated, "My intake of rum exactly matches my output of words." This fiery reporter would make a fascinating dinner guest. Anyone who would counsel a skinny young man to gain weight by drinking a daily bottle of beer for 120 days would surely be able to stir up some controversy over dinner!

Eggplant Casserole

This hearty main dish is useful for the meatless nights in your home, and it will also please the vegetarians in your club. It can be assembled in advance and refrigerated until baking time. The glossy-skinned eggplant was first cultivated by the Chinese in the fifth century BC and was grown in India for centuries, although it was unknown to the Greeks and Romans. Eggplants were brought to North America by the Spaniards.

1 1/2 lb	eggplant (about 1 large)	750 g
1/4 cup	all-purpose flour	50 mL
1 egg, lightly beaten		
2 tbsp	water	25 mL
1/2 tsp	salt	2 mL
3/4 cup	dried bread crumbs	175 mL
3–4 tbsp	olive oil	45–60 mL
1/2 lb	sliced mozzarella cheese	250 g
8 oz	tomato sauce (1 can)	228 mL
1/2 tsp	oregano	2 mL
1/2 cup	freshly grated Parmesan cheese	125 mL

1. Wash and cut the eggplant into slices about 1/2 to 3/4 inches (1 to 2 cm) thick; do not peel. Dredge slices with flour.

2. Combine egg, water and salt. Dip the floured pieces of eggplant in this mixture, then coat them with the bread crumbs. If time permits, refrigerate the slices for thirty minutes or longer to set the coating.

3. Preheat the oven to 400°F (200°C). Grease a shallow 2-quart (2-L) casserole dish or pan.

4. Heat two tablespoons of oil in a large skillet until hot but not smoking. Cook the eggplant slices slowing in the oil until tender, turning to brown both sides. Add more oil as needed.

5. Arrange the eggplant in a single layer in the casserole and distribute cheese slices over the top. Add 2 tbsp (25 mL) tomato sauce to each slice, and sprinkle with oregano and grated Parmesan cheese.

6. Bake until cheese melts, about 10 minutes.

Serves 6.

Cheese — milk's leap toward immortality.

Clifton Faidman,
Anyone Can Play,
1957

Maritime Blueberry Pudding

This authentic Maritime recipe comes straight from the kitchens of the Rock. It was brought to SWIVEL by a student from Newfoundland living in Ottawa who was justifiably proud of her culinary heritage. Serve this pudding, either hot or at room temperature, with ice cream or plain yogurt.

1/4 cup	butter	50 mL
1/2 cup	granulated sugar	125 mL
1 egg, beaten		
2 tsp	fresh lemon juice	10 mL
1 1/4 cup	cake and pastry flour	300 mL
1 tsp	baking powder	5 mL
1/2 tsp	salt	2 mL
1/2 cup	milk	125 mL
1/2 tsp	vanilla	2 mL
1 1/2 cups	blueberries	375 mL

1. Preheat oven to 350°F (180°C). Lightly grease a cake pan.
2. Cream butter and sugar together. Add beaten egg and lemon juice.
3. In a separate bowl, combine flour, baking powder and salt. Add these to butter and sugar mixture, a third at a time, alternating with the milk. Stir in vanilla and add blueberries.
4. Pour the pudding mixture into a cake pan. Bake for about 40 to 45 minutes.

Serves 8.

Oatmeal Cookies

These delectable cookies can't be too thin.

1 cup	butter	250 mL
2/3 cup	brown sugar	150 mL
1 egg, beaten		
1 cup	all-purpose flour	250 mL
1 tsp	baking soda	5 mL
1 tsp	salt	5 mL
2 1/2 cups rolled oats		650 mL
1 tsp	vanilla	5 mL

1. Preheat oven to 350°F (180°C). Butter a cookie sheet.
2. Cream butter and sugar until well blended. Add egg and mix well.
3. In a separate bowl, combine flour, baking soda and salt. Add to butter mixture.
4. Add oatmeal and vanilla and mix thoroughly.
5. Roll dough into balls, place on the cookie sheet, and press with a fork. Bake until golden, about 12 minutes.

Makes about 2 dozen cookies.

∼

William Shakespeare,
MACBETH
(ca. 1603–1606)

I nominate Lady Macbeth as the hostess for this dinner party. She does very well at keeping things civilized, even when emotions and suspicions overflow. She knows the rules of mannerly coming and going. No candles or finger bowls, please.

∼

Baklava

Here's a Canadian version of a traditional Mediterranean treat. There are countless variations of this popular pastry. The Greeks, the Romans and the Turks all lay claim to its invention. The choice of nuts usually depended on local availability, and every region developed its own version of baklava. However, all seem to agree that the top layer must be crisp, light and fluffy, the nutty filling must be moist, and the bottom must be thin and syrupy. The delicate balance of nuts, butter and sugar is a perfect match for espresso or Turkish coffee. Baklava can be made in advance and kept covered in the refrigerator for several days.

2 cups	finely chopped nuts	500 mL
	(pecans, walnuts, almonds)	
1 cup	granulated sugar	250 mL
1/2 cup	melted butter	125 mL
8 sheets phyllo dough		
1/2 cup	melted butter	125 mL
1 cup	pure maple syrup, warmed	250 mL

1. Preheat oven to 275°F (140°C).
2. Combine nuts, sugar and 1/2 cup (125 mL) melted butter. Set aside.
3. Lay out a sheet of phyllo. Brush half the sheet lightly with melted butter. Fold this half over the unbuttered half and butter the fresh surface.
4. Spoon one-eighth of the nut mixture onto the phyllo and spread out evenly.
5. Roll the phyllo dough into a tube and place in a lightly buttered rectangular baking pan.

6. Repeat steps 3 to 5 with the remaining nut mixture and sheets of phyllo. When finished brush the tops of the eight tubes with the other 1/2 cup (125 mL) melted butter.

7. Bake until browned and crisp (approximately 45 to 50 minutes).

8. Remove from oven. Pour warmed maple syrup over the baklavas and let cool. Cut tubes into pieces and serve.

Makes 24 pieces.

The recipes of the Mediterranean "speak the language of sunshine tastes and textures, of lightness and fun. They celebrate recreational eating ... (that) brings smiles of contentment."

BYRON AYANOGLU,
SIMPLY MEDITERRANEAN
COOKING,
1998

Johnny Cake

Johnny cake is a form of corn bread that dates back to the 1700s as journey cake — *perhaps because it was a tasty bread that could be prepared quickly at the end of a journey. There are countless variations using scalded cornmeal that is either baked or fried. This versatile bread was served for breakfast, used to accompany a main course at lunch or dinner, served as dessert slathered with butter and syrup, or even used to stuff a turkey. This version makes a tasty dessert served with maple syrup.*

1 cup	cornmeal	250 mL
2 cups	all-purpose flour	500 mL
3 tsp	baking powder	15 mL
3/4 cup	butter	175 mL
1 cup	granulated sugar	250 mL
3 eggs, beaten		
1 1/4 cup	milk	300 mL
cinnamon (optional, for garnish)		

1. Preheat oven to 350°F (180°C). Grease an 8-in (2-L) cake pan.
2. Sift cornmeal, flour and baking powder together.
3. Mix butter and sugar in a separate bowl; add beaten eggs.
4. Stir in dry ingredients, alternating with milk. Pour into cake pan and sprinkle with cinnamon if desired.
5. Bake for 30 minutes or until a toothpick inserted in the centre comes out clean.
6. Cool on a rack and cut into squares.

Serves 8.

3/ COLD MOUNTAIN
GETTING THE DISCUSSION FLOWING

APPETIZERS

Spinach, Leek & Tomato Terrine
Fresh Figs with Rosemary Goat Cheese
Marinated Brussels Sprouts
Zucchini Tian (aka Titan)

MAIN COURSES

Pork with Apples & Sweet Potatoes
Crab & Corn Pancakes
with Sweet& Sour Sauce
Hamburger Soup
Black Bean Chili

DESSERTS

Apple Crisp
Carrot Cake with Cream Cheese Icing
Chocolate Pecan Pie
Rhubarb Sour Cream Pie

Rhubarb Cordial
Peach Chutney

ARGUING YOUR POINT

At each meeting, following our meal, we turn our attention to discussion of the book selected for the evening. As a group of teachers, we have no difficulty in arguing our views. However, we know that our strong opinions might well meet with resistance from other members. Hence, most members prepare something to get the discussion flowing. The discussion might focus on a particularly interesting or poignant passage that is read to the group or on questions that have occurred to individuals as they read. We do not prepare formal discussion questions since we have never found the need for them, but other less loquacious groups might wish to experiment with this strategy.

Focus questions can be found at the back of some editions of novels, and a number of sample questions are given in the sidebars of this chapter.

THE INTREPID SURFER

If you are looking for information about a specific title on the Internet, one of the fastest ways to find a variety of sites is to enter the book title (usually in quotation marks — for example, "Cold Mountain") into a search engine such as Google or Alta Vista. You will likely find synopses and criticism, and you may well find someone else out there who shares your opinion!

Spinach, Leek & Tomato Terrine

This attractive appetizer is easier to prepare than it looks!

SPINACH LAYER

1 lb	fresh spinach, washed and stems removed	500 g
2 eggs, lightly beaten		
1/8 tsp	ground nutmeg	.5 mL
coarse salt and freshly ground black pepper (to taste)		

LEEK LAYER

1 lb	leeks (white part only)	500 g
2/3 cup	whipping cream	150 mL
1/4 tsp	dried thyme	1 mL
2 eggs, lightly beaten		
coarse salt and freshly ground black pepper (to taste)		

TOMATO LAYER

1 small onion, finely chopped		
2 large cloves garlic, minced		
2 tsp	butter	10 mL
28 oz can	plum tomatoes (processed in a food mill)	796 mL
1/2 tsp	dried basil	2 mL
2 eggs, lightly beaten		
coarse salt and freshly ground black pepper (to taste)		

How is character developed and revealed in the work: by what the characters say, by what they do, by what others say about them or by direct description? Think of Golding's LORD OF THE FLIES *(1954) or* W.O. Mitchell's WHO HAS SEEN THE WIND? *(1947).*

SPINACH LAYER

1. Wilt spinach in a little boiling water, but do not cook so long that it loses its fresh green colour. Drain and cool, then squeeze out excess moisture.
2. Finely chop spinach and mix with eggs and nutmeg. Season with salt and pepper. Divide mixture in half and set aside.

LEEK LAYER

1. Trim green off leeks, wash well and finely chop. Place in a skillet with cream and thyme. Simmer over medium heat until cream is reduced and mixture is dry. Allow to cool.
2. Stir eggs into leek mixture. Season with salt and pepper and set aside.

TOMATO LAYER

1. Sauté onion and garlic in butter until onion is soft. Add tomatoes and basil and simmer until no liquid remains.
2. Add eggs and season with salt and pepper. Set aside.

TO ASSEMBLE:

1. Preheat oven to 350°F (180°C). Line a terrine mould with parchment paper.
2. Spread half the spinach mixture on the bottom. Cover with all the leek mixture, then all the tomato mixture. Top with the remaining spinach mixture.
3. Cover with parchment paper and wrap the terrine in foil. Place in a roasting pan half filled with hot water. Bake for 2 hours, checking the water level occasionally to make sure the pan does not boil dry. Remove the terrine from the oven. Place a weight on top of the terrine to press out the liquid as it cools.

Serves 12.

Fresh Figs with Rosemary Goat Cheese

If fresh figs are not available, spread crackers with fig or peach preserves and use less honey with the goat cheese. The goat cheese mixture can be made a day ahead and chilled in the refrigerator. Bring it to room temperature before serving.

1 1/4 cups soft mild goat cheese, at room temperature		300 g
1/2 cup	35% cream	125 mL
2 tsp	finely chopped fresh rosemary	10 mL
1 tbsp	honey	15 mL
salt and pepper (to taste)		
1 lb	fresh figs	500 g

1. In a bowl, whisk together goat cheese, cream, rosemary and honey until smooth. Season with salt and pepper.
2. Mound goat cheese in the centre of a platter. Halve figs and arrange around the edge for dipping.

Makes 1 3/4 cups (425 mL).

To what degree is the central character working out some universal human problem? What is the nature of the problem? Think of Shakespeare's HAMLET (ca. 1599–1600) or Margaret Laurence's THE STONE ANGEL (1964).

Marinated Brussels Sprouts

These green morsels are surprisingly delicious. Prepare them the day before so that they can marinate for a full twenty-four hours.

1 lb	small firm Brussels sprouts	500 g
1/2 tsp	fresh dill	2 mL
1/2 cup	thinly sliced green onions	125 mL
1 cup	Italian-French dressing (recipe follows)	250 mL

1. Wash sprouts. Trim bottoms and remove loose leaves.
2. Cook in salted boiling water until almost tender (8 to 10 minutes).
3. Drain in a colander and chill quickly under cold running water. Drain and pat dry.
4. Arrange sprouts in a single layer in a flat dish. Sprinkle with dill and minced onions. Pour dressing over the sprouts. Cover tightly and marinate for 24 hours, turning once or twice.

Makes 8 appetizer servings.

ITALIAN-FRENCH DRESSING

1/4 cup	lemon juice	50 mL
1/4 cup	water	50 mL
3/4 cup	canola oil	175 mL
1 tbsp	ketchup	15 mL
1 tsp	paprika	5 mL
1 tsp	salt	5 mL
1/4 tsp	garlic salt	1 mL
1/4 tsp	black pepper	1 mL
1/4 tsp	dry mustard	1 mL

Combine all ingredients in a jar with a tight-fitting lid. Shake to blend. This dressing will keep 3 to 4 days in the refrigerator.

Makes about 1 cup (250 mL).

Which character or characters can you view sympathetically? Why? Remember Huck Finn's intelligent courage.

Zucchini Tian

The rich Mediterranean flavours of this vegetable dish —
a.k.a. Zucchini Titan — provide a Provençal link in the meal.
For best results, try to find young, slender zucchini.

2 cups	stale bread cubes	500 mL
hot water (enough to cover bread)		
1/4 cup	olive oil	50 mL
1/2 cup	chopped onion	125 mL
2 cloves garlic, minced		
1/2 cup	finely chopped red pepper	125 mL
2 green zucchini, thinly sliced		
2 yellow zucchini, thinly sliced		
2 tbsp	chopped fresh basil or coriander	25 mL
2 tbsp	chopped fresh parsley	25 mL
salt and pepper (to taste)		
pinch cayenne		
1/2 cup	freshly grated Parmesan cheese	125 mL
1 egg, lightly beaten		
1 tbsp	olive oil	15 mL

1. Preheat oven to 350°F (180°C). Oil a 2-quart (2-L) baking dish.

2. Put bread cubes in a bowl and cover with hot water. Set aside.

3. Heat oil over medium heat and sauté onion and garlic until soft. Add red pepper and cook for 3 more minutes. Remove from skillet and set aside.

4. Turn heat to high and add the zucchini to the skillet. Cook, turning constantly (watch that it does not burn). When

Do you find the conflicts presented in the work engaging? Are any or all of them resolved to your satisfaction? Consider Harper Lee's To Kill a Mockingbird *(1960) or any Hemingway novel.*

browned, remove from heat and stir into sautéd onion, garlic and red pepper.

5. Squeeze water from bread (don't worry about its paste-like consistency) and place in a large bowl. Add zucchini mixture, basil, parsley, salt and pepper, cayenne, cheese and egg. Mix well.

6. Place in baking dish and drizzle 1 tbsp (15 mL) of oil over the top. Bake 30 to 40 minutes or until a knife inserted in the centre comes out clean. If carrying as a potluck dish, bake for 30 mintues. Reheat, covered, for 10 minutes in a 350°F (180°C) oven.

Serves 6.

Pork with Apples & Sweet Potatoes

This rich warm casserole has all the right flavours and is perfect for a cold winter night.

1 tbsp	canola oil	15 mL
2 tbsp	butter	25 mL
2 lbs	lean pork, cut into chunks	1 kg
5 tbsp	all-purpose flour	75 mL
1 onion, chopped		
3 cooking apples, peeled, cored and sliced		
4–5 cups	unsweetened cider	about 1 L
4 chicken bouillon cubes		
1 tbsp	Dijon mustard	15 mL
3–4 medium-sized sweet potatoes, peeled and cubed		
freshly ground pepper (to taste)		
apple slices (for garnish)		

1. Preheat oven to 350°F (180°C). Lightly grease a shallow 2-quart (2-L) casserole dish.

2. Heat oil and butter in a large frying pan. Dredge pork pieces in flour and sauté until brown. Add onion and cook until soft. Place mixture in casserole dish.

3. In the same pan, lightly sauté apple slices until golden brown but still somewhat crunchy. Set aside.

4. Pour cider into pan and stir. Add bouillon cubes and mustard. Stir until cubes dissolve and the mixture is hot. Pour over pork and onion mixture.

&

What point of view is used in the work? What is the relationship in time and place between the narrator of the story and the action? How reliable is the narrator? Remember Nellie Dean in WUTHERING HEIGHTS *(1847) or Holden Caulfield in* THE CATCHER IN THE RYE *(1951).*

&

5. Cover casserole and bake for 1 1/2 hours.

6. Add sweet potatoes and ground pepper to casserole. Cover and bake for an additional 20 minutes or until the potatoes are soft. Remove from oven.

7. Decorate casserole with apple slices and serve. If carrying as a potluck dish, do not add the apple slices until after the dish has been reheated, in either a microwave or a traditional oven.

Serves 6 to 8.

Crab and Corn Pancakes with Sweet & Sour Sauce

This delightful dish features unusual combinations.

SWEET AND SOUR SAUCE

1 cup	tomato juice	250 mL
1 tbsp	brown sugar	15 mL
2 tsp	rice vinegar	25 mL
1 tbsp	minced ginger root	15 mL
1 tbsp	grated horseradish	15 mL
1 tsp	cornstarch	5 mL
1 tbsp	chopped cilantro	15 mL

CRAB AND CORN PANCAKES

4 oz	fresh or frozen crab meat	125 g
1 cup	fresh or frozen corn kernels	250 mL
2 large eggs, lightly beaten		
2 tbsp	cream or milk	25 mL
6 tbsp	all-purpose flour	90 mL
2 tsp	baking powder	10 mL
salt and pepper (to taste)		
1 tbsp	vegetable oil	15 mL
1 tbsp	butter	15 mL

1. In a small pan over medium heat, combine tomato juice, brown sugar, rice vinegar, ginger root and horseradish. Bring to a boil.

Where does the action take place? Are there few settings or many? What effects are created by changes in setting? For example, think of works by William Faulkner, which share a single setting, as opposed to a novel such as Anne Michael's FUGITIVE PIECES *(1996), which moves from continent to continent over two generations.*

2. Reduce heat to simmer. Dissolve cornstarch in 2 tbsp (25 mL) cold water, add to pan, and stir until thickened. Add cilantro and mix well. Remove from heat and set aside.

3. Combine crab and corn in mixing bowl. Add eggs, cream, flour and baking powder. Season with salt and pepper and mix well.

4. In a non-stick skillet heat oil and butter. Spoon batter into pan to make 4 pancakes. Cook 2 to 3 minutes per side or until golden.

5. Serve warm, topped with sauce. If carrying as a potluck dish, place pancakes on a cookie sheet and cover lightly with foil. Reheat at 325°F (160°C) for 10 minutes.

Serves 4.

Hamburger Soup

This soup is thick enough to eat with a fork! Leave it to simmer for as long as you want. The soup can also be made ahead of time and frozen. If you like a stronger herb flavour, increase the amounts of thyme, oregano and basil. Please note that you should always check with the host before planning to bring soup to a potluck — bowls might be a problem.

2 tbsp	olive oil	25 mL
1 1/2 lbs	lean ground beef	750 g
1 medium onion, finely chopped		
28 oz	can tomatoes	796 mL
2 cups	water	500 mL
30 oz	canned consommé (3 regular cans)	852 mL
4 carrots, finely cut		
1 bay leaf		
3 sticks celery, finely chopped		
1 clove garlic, minced		
1/2 tsp	thyme	2 mL
1/2 tsp	oregano	2 mL
1/2 tsp	basil	2 mL
pepper (to taste)		
6 tbsp	pot barley	90 mL

1. Heat oil in a large soup pot. Add beef and onions and cook until both are browned.
2. Add all remaining ingredients and stir to combine. Bring to a boil, cover and leave to simmer for at least 2 hours, and as long as all day.

Serves 10.

How does the author handle the time element: through flashbacks, foreshadowing, historical references or direct statements? For example, in ULYSSES *(1918), James Joyce takes about 700 pages to cover twenty-four hours. In* THE STONE DIARIES *(1993), Carol Shields dates each chapter. Margaret Laurence uses flashbacks to develop the plot of* THE STONE ANGEL *(1964) chronologically.*

Black Bean Chili

This recipe is a vegetarian treat, but if you want to please meat lovers, add ground beef sautéed with onions and garlic.

1 cup	chopped onion	250 mL
2 cloves garlic, minced		
1 tbsp	canola oil	15 mL
19 oz	can black beans	540 mL
28 oz	can tomatoes	796 mL
12 oz	can corn niblets	375 mL
2 tbsp	chili powder	25 mL
1 tbsp	ground cumin	15 mL
1 tsp	granulated sugar	5 mL
1 cup	chopped green and red peppers	250 mL
1 cup	sliced mushrooms	250 mL

1. In a large pot, sauté onions and garlic in oil until soft. Add beans, tomatoes, corn, chili powder, cumin and sugar. Cover and simmer 20 to 30 minutes.
2. Add peppers and mushrooms and simmer for 5 to 10 minutes.

Serves 4 to 6.

Apple Crisp

This is like the dessert your mother made, or perhaps even better!

3 lbs	apples	1 1/2 kg
1 1/2 cups	rolled oats	375 mL
1/4 cup	all-purpose flour	50 mL
2 cups	brown sugar, lightly packed	500 mL
1 cup	unsalted butter, chilled and cut into 12 pieces	250 mL
1 1/2 tsp	cinnamon	7 mL
pinch salt		
grated zest of 1 orange		

1. Preheat oven to 350°F (180°C).

2. Peel and core apples and cut into eighths. You should have about 10 cups (2.5 L).

3. Place oats, flour and 1 1/2 cups (375 mL) brown sugar in the bowl of a food processor. Process briefly to blend. (Do not overmix — you want the texture of the oats. The mixture should look dry.)

4. In a large bowl, combine apples, remaining 1/2 cup (125 mL) brown sugar, cinnamon, salt and orange zest. Toss until well mixed.

5. Spread apple mixture in a 13x9-inch (3.5-L) glass or earthenware baking dish. Cover evenly with the oat topping and pat gently.

6. Bake in the centre of the oven until the topping is golden and the fruit is bubbling, about 45 minutes. Cool to room temperature before serving.

Serves 8 to 10.

Carrot Cake with Cream Cheese Icing

This hearty cake is as traditional as it is flavourful. For a different icing, substitute 1 tbsp (15 mL) orange juice for the vanilla.

CARROT CAKE

1 1/2	cups oil	375 mL
2 cups	granulated sugar	500 mL
4 eggs		
2 cups	all-purpose flour	500 mL
2 tsp	baking powder	10 mL
1 1/2 tsp	baking soda	7 mL
1 tsp	salt	5 mL
2 tbsp	cinnamon	25 mL
2 cups	grated carrot	500 mL
1 cup	crushed pineapple	250 mL
1 1/2 cups	chopped walnuts	375 mL
1 tsp	vanilla	5 mL
Cream Cheese Icing (recipe follows)		

1. Preheat oven to 350°F (180°C). Grease and flour one 9-inch (2.5-L) springform pan.
2. Combine oil and sugar and mix with electric beater. Add eggs, one at a time.
3. In a separate bowl, combine flour, baking powder, baking soda, salt and cinnamon. Add to egg mixture, beating thoroughly.

What is the ratio of dialogue to narrative in the work? What is the effect of this ratio? Think about how dialogue informs readers of Sheila Watson's DOUBLE HOOK *(1959) or Roddy Doyle's* BARRYTOWN TRILOGY *(1988–1991).*

Stir in carrot, pineapple, walnuts and vanilla.

4. Pour batter into pan. Bake for 45 to 60 minutes or until a skewer inserted into the centre comes out clean.

5. Remove cake from pan and set on rack.

CREAM CHEESE ICING

8 oz	cream cheese, at room temperature	250 g
1/4 cup	butter, at room temperature	50 mL
2 1/2 cups	icing sugar	625 mL
2 tsp	vanilla (or 1 tbsp/15 mL orange juice)	10 mL

Soften cheese and butter and beat well to combine. Add sugar and vanilla or orange juice and beat again until smooth. Spread on cooled carrot cake.

Serves 16.

Which qualities of a woman described in the historical work are most striking and reminiscent of someone the reader knows today? Think of THE NEW DAY RECALLED: LIVES OF GIRLS AND WOMEN IN ENGLISH CANADA, 1919-1939 *(1998).*

Chocolate Pecan Pie

This stunning pie will provide a rich and delicious finale to any meal.

1 cup	butter	250 mL
1 cup	brown sugar	250 mL
2 cups	dark corn syrup	500 mL
6 extra large eggs		
10-inch	unbaked pie shell	25 cm
1 cup	chocolate chips	250 mL
2 cups	chopped toasted pecans	500 mL
12 toasted whole large pecans (for garnish)		

1. Preheat oven to 425°F (220°C).

2. Melt butter by microwaving for 30 seconds. Add sugar and corn syrup and beat together well by hand. Allow mixture to cool (this is important).

3. Beat eggs well and add to cooled butter mixture. Pour into pie shell. Sprinkle half of the chocolate chips over the surface and top with chopped pecans.

4. Bake pie on the bottom rack of the oven for approximately 10 minutes. Move pie to middle rack and reduce heat to 350°F (180°C). Continue baking for 1 to 1 1/4 hours. The pie is done when the filling is fairly firm — do not overbake or the filling will be dry.

5. To garnish with pecans, melt the remaining chocolate chips by microwaving for about 30 seconds. Dip the forked ends of the whole pecans into melted chocolate and set around the edge of the pie, about 1 inch (2.5 cm) apart, with the chocolate ends resting on the filling. Arrange four of the largest pecans in the centre as an extra garnish.

Serves 8.

As a reader, how do you respond to the structure (numbered sections, numbered chapters, titled sections, titled chapters or continuous prose) chosen by the author for this book?

Rhubarb Sour Cream Pie

This old-fashioned pie is at once tart and sweet.

4 cups	cubed rhubarb	1 L
1 1/2 cups	granulated sugar	375 mL
1/3 cup	all-purpose flour	75 mL
1 cup	sour cream	250 mL
1 unbaked pie shell		
1/2 cup	all-purpose flour	125 mL
1/2 cup	brown sugar	125 mL
1/4 cup	butter	50 mL

1. Preheat oven to 450°F (230°C).
2. Combine rhubarb, sugar and 1/3 cup (75 mL) flour, and mix well. Add sour cream. Place in pie shell.
3. Combine 1/2 cup (125 mL) flour, brown sugar and butter, and mix until crumbly. Sprinkle over top of rhubarb mixture.
4. Bake for 15 minutes. Reduce heat to 350°F (180°C) and continue baking for 30 minutes or until the fruit is tender and the filling is set. The topping should be golden brown.

Serves 5.

How much is your attention focused on seeking out the statement or paragraph which reveals the significance of the title? Consider SPADEWORK: A NOVEL *(2001) by Timothy Findey, or* THE HERO'S WALK *(2000) by Anita Rau Badami.*

Rhubarb Cordial

This simple drink is both colourful and refreshing. The drink base can be kept in the refrigerator for about a week. To serve, combine the base with approximately equal portions of water, soda water, sparkling mineral water or wine.

2 1/2 lbs	chopped rhubarb	1.5 kg
6 cups	water	1.5 L
1 cup	granulated sugar	250 mL

1. In a large stainless steel or enamel pot, combine rhubarb and water. Bring to a boil, reduce heat and simmer for 10 minutes or until soft. Strain through a dampened jelly bag or a sieve lined with cheesecloth, discarding pulp and preserving juice.

2. Rinse pot carefully and return juice. Add sugar and bring to a boil, stirring until the sugar is dissolved.

3. Pour juice into containers, cool and refrigerate.

Makes about 4 cups (1 L).

Peach Chutney

This recipe is quite unlike anything done with peaches in Cold Mountain.
*We recommend preserving this recipe so that the flavours combine, and it
makes a handy item in a well-stocked pantry.*

6	1-pint (500-mL) jars with lids
2 tsp	curry powder 10 mL
2 tbsp	celery seed 25 mL
1 tbsp	mustard seed 15 mL
6 1/2 lb	peaches 3 kg
2 cups	malt vinegar 500 mL
2 cups	brown sugar, lightly packed 500 mL
4 oz	chopped fresh gingerroot 125 g
2 medium onions, finely chopped	
2 green peppers, seeded and finely chopped	
1 hot banana pepper, seeded and finely chopped	
1 cup	dark raisins 250 mL
1 cup	golden raisins 250 mL
1 cup	mixed glazed peel 250 mL
1 tbsp	pickling salt 15 mL

1. Place the spices on a piece of cheesecloth, and tie up to create a spice bag.
2. To prepare jars for preserving, place 6 clean 1-pint (500-mL) jars and lids in a container large enough to hold them. Cover them with water and bring to a boil. (Wait until about 30 minutes into the cooking to do this. Lids and jars only boil for 5 minutes, maximum.)
3. Blanch, peel and pit peaches. Coarsely chop peaches, and

*Does the author's use
of sense appeal as a
descriptive device
include references to
the preparation and
serving of food?
Could you cook one
of the dishes and
bring it to the
book club?
Think of the menu for*
LARRY'S PARTY *(1997)
by Carol Shields.*

combine with vinegar in a large stainless steel or enamel saucepan. Stir in sugar. Bring to a boil and cook until peaches are tender.

4. Add spice bag, ginger root, onions, green and banana pepper, dark and golden raisins, mixed glazed peel and pickling salt to peaches. Stir to move spice bag around the pot. Return mixture to the boil, and stirring frequently, simmer until thick, about 45 minutes.

5. Remove thickened chutney from the heat, and discard spice bag.

6. Remove the jars from the hot water, shake off any excess water and ladle chutney into a hot jar to within 1/2 inch (1 cm) of top rim. Remove air bubbles by sliding rubber spatula between glass and food; readjust head space to 1/2 inch (1 cm). Wipe jar rims to remove stickiness, and seal.

7. Place the filled jars back into the container of water, cover with 2 inches (5 cm) of water and process in boiling-water bath for 10 minutes.

8. Remove, cool 24 hours, check seals, and store in cool dark place.

Makes 6 1-pint (500-mL) jars.

Section Two

ORGANIZING
BOOK CLUB MEETINGS
BY SINGLE AUTHOR

Invitations for SWIVEL meetings

4 / RODDY DOYLE

Favourite Authors Who Stir Debate

APPETIZERS

Smoked Salmon Mousse

Poor Man's Cheese en Croûte

MAIN COURSES

Traditional Irish Stew

Irish Colcannon

Templemore Baked Potatoes

Mussel & Potato Salad

Potato Cakes with Leeks & Carrots

DESSERTS

Coffee Cream Dessert

Old-Fashioned Figged Duff

Bread Pudding with Whiskey Sauce

Irish Brown Bread

RODDY DOYLE

NOVELS

The Barrytown Trilogy:
The Commitments, 1988
The Snapper, 1990
The Van, 1991
Paddy Clark Ha Ha Ha, 1993
The Woman Who Walked
into Doors, 1996
A Star Called Henry, 1999

PLAYS

Brownbread, 1992
War, 1993

FILMS

The Commitments, 1991
The Snapper, 1993
The Van, 1996

EXPANDING LITERARY HORIZONS

There have been several authors who so interested SWIVEL members that we devoted an evening to discussing their works. For such evenings, each member read one or more books by the featured author. In the case of Roddy Doyle, for example, some members read one of his first three novels, the humorous *Barrytown Trilogy* based on the lives of Irish working-class families, while others selected his award-winning *The Woman Who Walked into Doors.* We have found that our discussions about the merits and shortcomings of an author's "oeuvre" seem to have more focus than our debates about literary themes or genres. Although not everyone has necessarily read the same books, it is an easy and enlightening task to relate one specific example to a similar instance found in another work.

Another advantage of having members choose any book by an author is that it is usually fairly easy for each member to find something to read. (For once, the local library is not besieged by the entire club wanting the same title!) At meetings where each person may have read a different book, individual members give brief summaries in order to provide essential background for the rest of the group. Needless to say, well-told summaries often result in other members scribbling down the titles as "must reads."

The author for an "oeuvre" discussion should be carefully selected. The best candidates are those who have produced a wide variety of works. This allows for comparison of works written at several stages of the author's career or works written in different genres. Such comparative reading can become the basis for members' differing opinions. For example, at an evening devoted to Canadian author Matt Cohen, SWIVEL members were divided in their final assessment of Cohen's value as a writer but each member was able to draw on selections from a large body of work —

including novels, novelettes, short stories and literary reviews — to support firmly held views.

The menu for this chapter has an Irish theme (appropriate for a Roddy Doyle evening) and includes book lists for a number of authors whose collected works provide a suitable range for enlightened and lively discussion.

THE INTREPID SURFER

Search engines provide a quick way to find a number of Web sites devoted to a particular author. Enter the author's name to find interviews, bibliographies, summaries of works and even on-line shopping for books!

May you have warm words on a cold evening, a full moon on a dark night and the road downhill all the way to your door.

IRISH TOAST

Smoked Salmon Mousse

This mousse is as smooth as silk. For an elegant presentation, pipe it onto slices of Melba toast or rye bread. It can be made up to two days before serving.

7 oz	chopped smoked salmon	220 g
1 tsp	fresh lemon juice	5 mL
1/2 cup	10% cream	125 mL
1/4 cup	lightly whipped 35% cream	50 mL

1. Combine salmon and lemon juice in a blender or food processor, and blend for 2 minutes. Gradually pour in the 10% cream and continue to blend on low speed.
2. Transfer mixture to a bowl and, using a spatula, gently fold in the whipped cream. Cover with plastic wrap and refrigerate for 4 hours or until ready to serve.

Makes 8 appetizer servings.

Poor Man's Cheese en Croûte

This elegant time saver can be prepared in minutes!

8 oz	round Gouda cheese	250 g
8 oz pkg.	frozen crescent roll dough	250 g

1. Slice cheese into two rounds. Divide dough into two equal portions.
2. Wrap each portion of cheese in a portion of the dough, making sure that the cheese is completely covered.
3. Bake as directed on the dough package.

Serves 6 to 8.

Traditional Irish Stew

MATT COHEN

FICTION
Johnny Crackle Sings, 1971
The Disinherited, 1974
Wooden Hunters, 1975
The Colours of War, 1977
The Leaves of Louise, 1978
*The Sweet Second Summer
of Kitty Malone*, 1979
Flowers of Darkness, 1981
The Spanish Doctor, 1984
Nadine, 1986
Living on Water, 1988
Emotional Arithmetic,
1990
*Freud:
The Paris Notebooks*,
1991
The Bookseller, 1993
Last Seen, 1996
Elizabeth and After,
1999

*This is truly a traditional Irish stew. You can use beef bouillon —
either canned or in cubes — for the brown stock* (season the stock
to your liking with salt and pepper, dry sherry, lemon juice,
dry mustard and herbs). Just before serving the stew, top with
a little sour cream and chopped green onions.*

1/2 oz	whole allspice	15 g
1/2 oz	whole cloves	15g
1/2 oz	pickling spice	15 g
1–2 large bay leaves		
3–4 lbs	lamb	1–1.5 kg
flour for dredging lamb		
oil for browning lamb		
oil for sautéing leeks		
2 medium leeks, sliced		
3 large carrots, sliced		
1 bottle dark beer		
2 cups	*brown stock	500 mL
1/2 lb	pearl onions, peeled	250 g
2 lbs	potatoes, peeled and quartered	1 kg
1 cup	frozen peas	250 ml
sour cream (for garnish)		
chopped green onion (for garnish)		

1. Preheat oven to 350°F (180°C).
2. Tie up allspice, cloves, pickling spice and bay leaves in a small
   piece of cheesecloth to make a spice bag.

3. Cut lamb into 1-inch (2.75-cm) cubes. Working in batches, coat with a thin layer of flour and sear in a skillet with a little oil until browned. Remove meat from pan and place in a Dutch oven or an ovenproof casserole dish.

4. Using same skillet, cook leeks with enough oil until tender. Add to meat.

5. Pour beer into skillet, bring to a boil and stir until pan residue is loosened. Remove from heat and pour over the meat and leek mixture.

6. Add carrots, brown stock, and spice bag to the Dutch oven or casserole dish. Cover and bake for 1 hour.

7. Add pearl onions and potatoes and bake for 1 more hour or until tender. Add peas in the last 15 minutes. If the stew is not thick enough, stir in a small amount of flour mixed with water and simmer until thickened. Season with salt and pepper.

8. If carrying as a potluck dish, reheat, covered, for 10 to 15 minutes at 350°F (180°C) before serving. Garnish with sour cream and green onions.

Serves 6 to 8.

SHORT STORIES
Columbus and the Fat Lady, 1972
Night Flights, 1978
The Expatriate, 1982
Café le Dog, 1983
The Dream Class Anthology, 1983
Getting Lucky, 2000

BIOGRAPHY
Typing: A Life in 26 Keys, 2000

Irish Colcannon

Tradition, tradition! When eaten at Halloween, colcannon often contained a plain gold ring, a sixpence and a thimble or a button. The finder of the ring could expect to be married within the year; the sixpence meant wealth; the thimble foretold spinsterhood; and the button, bachelorhood.

5 medium potatoes		
2 tbsp	butter	25 mL
3 cups	shredded cabbage	750 mL
4 oz	cream cheese	125 g
3 green onions, sliced		
1 tsp	salt	5 mL
fresh ground pepper (to taste)		
1 tsp	caraway seeds	5 mL
1 cup	freshly grated Cheddar cheese	250 mL

1. Preheat oven to 425°F (220°C). Butter a 1-1/2-quart (1.5-L) casserole dish.

2. Cook potatoes until tender. Drain and mash with butter. Set aside.

3. Cook cabbage in boiling salted water until tender. Drain.

4. Mix together potatoes, cabbage, cream cheese and onions. Stir in salt, pepper and caraway seeds. Pour into casserole dish and sprinkle top with grated cheese.

5. Bake for 30 to 40 minutes or until bubbly and browned on top.

Serves 4.

Templemore Baked Potatoes

A surprising rendition. Templemore is the name of a town in south central Ireland known for its moated graveyard and ancient church ruins.

6 large potatoes, freshly baked		
1/4 cup	butter, softened	50 mL
1/4 cup	whiskey liqueur (optional)	50 mL
1 egg, beaten		
1 cup	sour cream	250 mL
2 tbsp	chives	25 mL
3/4 tsp	salt	4 mL
1/4 tsp	pepper	1 mL

1. Preheat oven to 400°F (200°C).
2. Slit potato skins and scoop out potato. Reserve the skins.
3. Combine hot potato, butter, liqueur (if using), egg, sour cream, chives, salt and pepper. Fill potato skins with this mixture.
4. Bake for 10 minutes.

Serves 6.

JOHN IRVING

NOVELS
Setting Free the Bears, 1968
The Water-Method Man, 1972
The 158-pound Marriage, 1974
The World According to Garp, 1978
The Hotel New Hampshire, 1981
The Cider House Rules, 1985
A Prayer for Owen Meany, 1989
A Son of the Circus, 1994
A Widow for One Year, 1998
The Fourth Hand, 2001

MEMOIRS
My Movie Business, 1999

FILMS
The World According to Garp, 1982
The Hotel New Hampshire, 1984
Simon Birch, 1998
The Cider House Rules, 1999

Mussel & Potato Salad

A tasty variation on a favourite old-fashioned standby.

4 lb	steamed mussels	2 kg
1/4 cup	lemon juice	50 mL
2 tbsp	finely chopped shallots	25 mL
1/4 cup	chopped fresh parsley	50 mL
1 1/2 lb	new potatoes	750 g
2 tbsp	dry white wine	25 mL
2/3 cup	olive or vegetable oil	150 mL
salt and pepper (to taste)		
1 egg (optional)		
1 tbsp	white wine vinegar	15 mL
1 1/2 tsp	minced fresh oregano (or 1/2 tsp/2 mL dried)	7 mL
1 1/2 tsp	Dijon mustard	7 mL
1/2 tsp	dry mustard	2 mL
2 hard-boiled eggs, cut in wedges		
chopped fresh parsley (for garnish)		
oak or other leaf lettuce (for salad base)		

1. Remove mussels from shells. In a large bowl, combine mussels, lemon juice, shallots and half of the parsley. Cover and refrigerate 1 hour.

2. Scrub potatoes. In a saucepan of boiling, salted water, cook potatoes until tender but firm. Drain and peel. If potatoes are large, cut in quarters; if tiny, leave whole.

3. In a bowl, combine warm potatoes with wine, 2 tbsp (25 mL) of oil, remaining parsley and salt and pepper. Marinate at room temperature for 30 to 60 minutes.

4. In a blender or food processor, combine egg (if using), vinegar, oregano, Dijon and dry mustards, and salt and pepper to taste. With machine running, gradually add remaining oil in a thin stream as the dressing thickens.

5. Combine mussel mixture, potato mixture and dressing; stir gently. Cover and refrigerate for about 2 hours to blend flavours.

6. To serve, line individual plates with lettuce. Mound salad on top and garnish with egg wedges and parsley.

Serves 8.

Potato Cakes with Leeks and Carrots

Garnish these delectable cakes with sour cream (if desired) and serve with a salad and some sausage for a hearty main course.

1 lb	russet potatoes, peeled and coarsely grated	500 g
1 cup	sliced leeks (white and pale green parts only)	250 mL
2/3 cup	coarsely grated peeled carrots	150 mL
salt and pepper		
4 tbsp	butter	60 mL
sour cream (optional, for garnish)		

1. Wrap grated potatoes in several layers of paper towels and squeeze dry. Place potatoes in large bowl. Add leeks and carrots and toss to combine. Season generously with salt and pepper.

2. Melt 2 tbsp (25 mL) butter in each of two heavy medium-size skillets over medium-low heat. Add half of the potato mixture (about 2 cups/500 mL) to each skillet. Using a spatula, flatten the potatoes in each skillet into a cake about 7–8 inches (18–20 cm) in diameter.

3. Cover skillets and cook until cakes are crisp and brown at the edges, about 12 minutes. Turn cakes and cook uncovered until the potatoes are cooked through and the cakes are crisp and brown on bottom, about 5 minutes longer. Transfer to plates.

4. The potato cakes can be prepared 3 hours ahead. If carrying as a potluck dish, transfer the cakes to a baking sheet and let stand at room temperature. Reheat in a 375°F (190°C) oven until crisp, about 10 minutes.

Serves 2 as a main dish.

Coffee Cream Dessert

This elegant dessert is quick and reliable, but requires a 12-hour setting time. Just before serving, dust with a mixture of cocoa and instant coffee granules. You can substitute an angel food cake or a sponge cake cut into 1-inch (5-cm) pieces for the ladyfingers.

30 ladyfingers		
1 cup	strong coffee	250 mL
2 tbsp	18% cream	25 mL
1/2 cup	unsalted butter	125 mL
1 cup	icing sugar	250 mL
4 eggs, separated		
1/2 tsp	vanilla	2 mL
1 tsp	instant coffee granules (or to taste)	5 mL
1/2 cup	toasted slivered almonds	125 mL

1. Line a large bowl with ladyfingers. Combine coffee and cream, and pour over ladyfingers. Let soak for 10 minutes. The ladyfingers will soak up most, if not all, of the liquid.

2. Meanwhile, make the filling. Cream butter and icing sugar together until fluffy. Add egg yolks, one at a time, beating well after each addition. Mix until smooth. Add vanilla and instant coffee.

3. Beat egg whites until stiff. Fold egg whites and almonds into filling mixture.*

4. Spread filling over ladyfingers in the bowl. Cover with plastic wrap and chill for 12 hours or more before serving.

Serves 6 to 8.

* If you have food safety concerns about uncooked eggs,
  see note on page 168.

* If you have food safety concerns about uncooked eggs, see note on page 168.

❧

JANE URQUHART

FICTION
The Whirlpool, 1986
Changing Heaven, 1990
Away, 1993
The Underpainter, 1997
The Stone Carvers,
2001

SHORT STORIES
Storm Glass,
1987

POETRY
*I Am Walking in
the Garden of His
Imaginary Palace,* 1981
False Shuttles, 1982
*The Little Flowers of
Madame de Montespan,*
1983
Some Other Garden,
2000

❧

Old-Fashioned Figged Duff

Here's a Newfoundland version of an Irish favourite.

6–8 slices	stale bread with crusts	
1 cup	warm water	250 mL
1 cup	raisins	250 mL
1/2 cup	brown sugar	125 mL
pinch salt		
1 tsp	each ginger, allspice, cinnamon	5 mL
1 tsp	baking soda	5 mL
1 tbsp	hot water	15 mL
1/4 cup	melted butter	50 mL
3 tbsp	molasses	45 mL
1/2 cup	sifted all-purpose flour	125 mL
1/2 cup	molasses, warmed	125 mL

1. Soak stale bread in 1 cup (250 mL) water for a few minutes. Squeeze out the water and rub bread between hands to make crumbs. Measure out 3 cups (750 mL) without pressing down into the cup. Place in a medium-size bowl.

2. Combine raisins, sugar, salt, ginger, allspice and cinnamon with bread crumbs.

3. Dissolve baking soda in hot water. Add melted butter, 3 tbsp (45 mL) molasses and the baking soda to the bread crumb mixture. Add the flour and mix well.

4. Lightly oil an 8-cup (2-L) mould. Turn batter into the mould and cover with a double layer of heavy foil. Tie tightly with string.

Place on a rack in a deep pot and add boiling water until water reaches halfway up the pan. Cover. Bring to a boil, then reduce heat to a simmer. Steam for 1 1/2–2 hours or until pudding is done. Replenish water if necessary. Turn out of mould immediately and allow to cool.

5. Serve with 1/2 cup (125 mL) warmed molasses.

Serves 6.

Bread Pudding with Whiskey Sauce

Serve this delicious microwave item with Whiskey Sauce (if possible), whipped cream or ice cream. If you want a browned top, put the pudding under the broiler for a minute or two.

4 cups	1/2-inch (1 cm) cubes of day-old French bread 1 L
1/3 cup	dark raisins 75 mL
3/4 cup	pecan halves 175 mL
6 tbsp	granulated sugar 90 mL
1 1/2 tsp	butter 7 mL
1/2 tsp	cinnamon 2 mL
dash freshly ground nutmeg	
2 cups	light cream or homogenized milk 500 mL
2 eggs, lightly beaten	
Whiskey Sauce (recipe follows)	

1. Butter an 8-inch (20-cm) round glass baking dish. Layer bread cubes, raisins and pecans in the dish.

2. Combine sugar, butter, cinnamon, nutmeg and cream in a 4-cup (1-L) glass measure. Stir to mix well. Microwave on medium for 3 to 4 minutes, or until butter melts and cream is warm. Quickly whisk in eggs.

3. Pour the cream mixture over the bread in the pan. Sprinkle with a little more cinnamon.

4. Cover with microwave-safe plastic wrap. Microwave covered on medium for 10 minutes, then uncovered for 1 to 2 minutes

more, or until pudding is set almost to the centre.
Let stand 5 minutes.

5. Serve warm with Whiskey Sauce.

Serves 4 to 6.

WHISKEY SAUCE

Since this sauce separates as it cools it must be served at once, and is therefore not suitable for a potluck unless it can be made on the spot.

6 tbsp	butter	90 mL
1/2 cup	granulated sugar	125 mL
1 egg		
1/4 cup	Irish whiskey	50 mL

1. Melt butter in a double-boiler over hot but not boiling water.

2. Whisk sugar and egg together in a small bowl. Slowly whisk egg mixture into the melted butter. Cook and stir until sauce thickens slightly.

3. Remove from heat and stir in whiskey. Serve at once.

Makes about 1 cup (250 mL).

May the roof above us never fall in, and may we friends gathered below never fall out.

IRISH TOAST

Irish Brown Bread

This versatile, tasty bread can be served with smoked fish as an appetizer or used to soak up the juices of an Irish stew.

OLIVER SACKS

British-trained neurologist who wrote vivid descriptions of neurological conditions, their physical manifestations and the coping strategies used by those afflicted.

Migraine, 1970
A Leg to Stand On, 1984
The Man Who Mistook His Wife for a Hat, 1985
Seeing Voices, 1989
Awakenings, 1990
An Anthropologist on Mars, 1995
The Island of the Colorblind, 1996
Uncle Tungsten: Memories of a Chemical Boyhood, 2001

1 3/4 cups	all-purpose flour	425 mL
1 3/4 cups	whole wheat flour	425 mL
3 tbsp	toasted wheat bran	45 mL
3 tbsp	toasted wheat germ	45 mL
2 tbsp	old-fashioned oats	25 mL
2 tbsp	dark brown sugar, packed	25 mL
1 tsp	baking soda	5 mL
1/2 tsp	salt	2 mL
2 tbsp	chilled unsalted butter, cut into pieces	25 mL
2 cups	buttermilk	500 mL

1. Preheat oven to 425°F (220°C). Butter a 9x5-inch (2-L) loaf pan.
2. Combine flours, wheat bran, wheat germ, oats, sugar, baking soda and salt in large bowl. Mix well. Add butter and rub in with fingertips until the mixture resembles fine meal.
3. Stir in enough buttermilk to form soft dough. Transfer dough to prepared loaf pan.
4. Bake until bread is dark brown and a tester inserted into centre comes out clean, about 40 minutes.
5. Turn bread out of pan and cool right side up on a rack.

Makes 1 loaf.

5/ PAT BARKER

From the Writer's Hand

APPETIZERS

Tomato Soup

Devilled Eggs

Chèvre and Tapenade Appetizer

MAIN COURSES

Newfoundland Hash

Coq au Vin

Curried Broccoli & Shrimp Salad

Seafood Casserole

DESSERTS

Lemon Charlotte Russe
with Raspberry Sauce

Yorkshire Parkin

Strawberry Shortcake

Dundee Cake

WRITING THE PAST

Pat Barker, one of the leading voices in British writing, has published eight novels since 1982. Born in 1943, she was raised by her working-class grandparents in northern industrial England. She read history at the London School of Economics, taught school, raised two children and, after a long effort, achieved publication in 1982 with her novel *Union Street*. In the early 1990s her *Regeneration Trilogy* garnered praise from the *New York Times Book Review*. The second book of this trilogy won the Guardian Fiction Prize, and the third book won the Booker Award.

NOVELS
Union Street, 1982
This novel portrays the difficult and precarious lives of seven women in a factory neighbourhood of industrial England. The film *Stanley & Iris* (1989) is based on the novel.

Blow Your House Down, 1984
This novel continues the themes of *Union Street* but with a darker vision of prostitutes' lives in a grim industrial town.

Liza's England, 1986 (former title, *The Century's Daughter*)
The story of a working-class woman's life in twentieth-century Britain is told from the viewpoint of eighty-year old Liza Wright.

The Man Who Wasn't There, 1989
In this novel, Barker's imagination switches to describing the world of a fatherless teenage boy growing up in 1950s England.

THE REGENERATION TRILOGY
Regeneration, 1992
The Eye in the Door, 1993 — winner of the 1993 Guardian Fiction Prize
The Ghost Road, 1995 — winner of the 1995 Booker Award

The *Regeneration Trilogy* is a brilliant and powerful description of the First World War and its cruel impact on the young men who fought in the horror of the trenches. The action revolves around the real-life relationship between the eminent British poet Siegfried Sassoon and Dr. William Rivers, an army psychologist who specialized in shell shock.

Another World, 1998
Life in modern Britain is experienced by Geordie, a centenarian war veteran, Nick, a middle-aged school teacher, and Gareth, the eleven-year old stepson of Nick. It is a novel of memory and identity and "the power of old wounds to leak into the present."

THE INTREPID SURFER

You can search the files of the prestigious *New York Times Book Review* at www.nytimes.com/books by entering the title of a book or the name of an author. The Intrepid Surfer also recommends the Contemporary Authors series at your local public library.

QUOTATIONS

I always have a quotation for everything — it saves original thinking.

DOROTHY L. SAYERS,
HAVE HIS CARCASE, 1932

Many writers, readers and conversationalists love quotations. The writers' quotations in this chapter's sidebars, like a shake of salt to season the broth, comment on the writing process and the joy of reading. Most readers are curious about the creative process, and are delighted and sometimes pleasantly shocked to discover in a writer's musings a kindred spirit who expresses what they themselves have experienced or thought.

The role of the writer is not to say what we can all say, but what we are unable to say.

ANAÏS NIN,
THE DIARY OF ANAÏS NIN,
VOL.5,
1974

Tomato Soup

This tasty soup brings sun-ripened warmth to a cold winter evening.

SOUP BASE

The proportion of tomatoes to the other ingredients combined should be about four to one.

chopped onion, celery
chopped peppers (optional)
garlic (to taste)
olive oil
ripe tomatoes, cored, seeded and chopped

SOUP

Use equal quantities of soup base and other liquid:
cream, milk or chicken stock
salt and pepper (to taste)

1. Make the soup base. In an enamel or stainless steel pot, sauté onion, celery, garlic and peppers (if using) in oil until softened. Add tomatoes. Cover and simmer for about 45 minutes or until vegetables are very soft.

2. Line a sieve with cheesecloth and press the tomato mixture through. Reserve the liquid soup base.

3. Make the soup. Heat soup base gently. Add other liquid and continue heating. Do not allow the mixture to boil. Taste and correct seasoning.

Servings will vary, depending on the amount of tomato used.

Soup not only warms you and is easy to swallow and to digest, it also creates an illusion in the back of your mind that Mother is there.

MARLENE DIETRICH,
*MARLENE DIETRICH'S
ABC,* 1962

Devilled Eggs

Garnish these colourful appetizers with chopped chives, chopped parsley, diced pimento, minced red pepper or a shake of paprika.

6 hard-boiled eggs		
2/3 cup	**mayonnaise**	**150 mL**
1/2 tsp	**salt**	**2 mL**
1/4 tsp	**pepper**	**1 mL**
1/2 tsp	**dry mustard**	**2 mL**
2 green onions, finely chopped		

1. Cut hard-boiled eggs in half lengthwise. Slip out yolks into small mixing bowl and mash with a fork. Blend in mayonnaise, salt, pepper, mustard and onions.
2. Pack egg-yolk mixture into egg whites, heaping lightly. Garnish and serve.

Makes 12 devilled eggs.

No entertainment is so cheap as reading, nor any pleasure so lasting.

LADY MARY WORTLEY MONTAGU, IN A LETTER TO HER DAUGHTER LADY BUTE, JUNE 22, 1752

Chèvre and Tapenade Appetizer

This heady combination of Mediterranean flavours is bound to add warmth and joy to an evening gathering. If you're short of time, ready-made tapenade is available at most large grocery stores or in specialty food shops.

4 1/2 oz	chèvre	140 g
1 tbsp	olive oil	15 mL
1 clove garlic, minced		
salt and freshly ground pepper (to taste)		
1 baguette		
1/4 cup	Tapenade (recipe follows)	50 mL
2 roasted red peppers, sliced		
8 large fresh basil leaves		

1. Combine chèvre, olive oil, garlic, salt and pepper. Set aside.

2. Cut baguette in half lengthwise and scoop out the centre of bread leaving a thin layer attached to the crust. Reserve scooped-out bread for another use.

3. Spread one half of the baguette with tapenade and top with pieces of red pepper. Spread the second half with the cheese mixture and top with the basil leaves.

4. Sandwich baguette halves together and wrap tightly with plastic wrap. Refrigerate until serving time.

5. To serve, slice into 1/2-inch (1-cm) slices.

Makes 30 to 35 pieces.

TAPENADE

Tapenade, a combination of typical Provençal ingredients, can be spread on toast, used as a condiment or served with crudités. The general rule is to use a few more olives than capers and anchovies, but individual cooks adjust the recipe according to personal taste. Add pepper, but use very little salt. Tapenade can also be flavoured with garlic, bay leaves, thyme, mustard and even rum or brandy.

pitted black olives, salt-cured but unflavoured
anchovy fillets, washed free of salt or use oil-cured
capers
salt and pepper to taste
mild extra-virgin olive oil

Mash olives, anchovies and capers with a mortar and pestle. Add pepper and salt. Drizzle in oil, mixing until the paste becomes creamy. Add other flavourings as desired.

I try to live what I consider a "poetic existence." That means I take responsibility for the air I breathe and the space I take up. I try to be immediate, to be totally present for all my work.

MAYA ANGELOU,
BLACK WOMEN WRITERS AT WORK, ED. CLAUDIA TATE,
1983

Newfoundland Hash

Who'd think it was leftovers?

2 cups	ground or finely chopped cooked meat	500 mL
3 cups	diced cooked potatoes	750 mL
1 onion, chopped		
1 tsp	salt	5 mL
1 tbsp	sweet green relish	15 mL
1 tbsp	ketchup	15 mL
1–2 tbsp	milk	15–25 mL
1/4 cup	grated Cheddar cheese	50 mL
1/4 cup	cracker crumbs	50 mL
2 tbsp	butter	25 mL

1. Preheat oven to 400°F (200°C). Grease an 8-inch (2-L) baking dish.
2. Combine meat, potatoes, onion, salt, relish and ketchup. Mix well. Moisten with milk.
3. Spread mixture in baking dish. The layer should be about 1-inch (2.5-cm) thick. Cover with grated cheese and cracker crumbs, and dot with butter.
4. Bake for 40 minutes. If carrying as a potluck dish, reheat in a microwave oven.

Serves 4.

I never see any home cooking. All I get is fancy stuff.

PRINCE PHILIP,
DUKE OF EDINBURGH
THE OBSERVER,
DECEMBER 1962

Coq au Vin

This tasty chicken recipe can be served with either rice or noodles, and the flavours blend well if it is prepared ahead of time and reheated before serving. To remove skins from pearl onions easily, soak them in hot water for two or three minutes. You can substitute 1/2 cup (125 mL) chopped scallions for the shallots.

3 1/2–4 lbs chicken pieces (broilers or fryers)		1.5–2 kg
salt and freshly ground black pepper (to taste)		
1/2 cup	diced salt pork or bacon	125 mL
2 tbsp	butter	25 mL
1/2 lb	pearl onions, peeled	250 g
1/2 lb	mushrooms	250 g
2–3 shallots, chopped		
1 clove garlic, minced		
2 tbsp	all-purpose flour	25 mL
2 cups	dry red wine	500 mL
3 sprigs parsley		
1/2 bay leaf		
1/8 tsp	thyme	.5 mL
2 tbsp	chopped parsley	25 mL

1. Season the chicken pieces with salt and pepper.
2. If using salt pork, parboil for five minutes, then drain and sauté in butter until brown. If using bacon, sauté until cooked. Remove from pan and set aside. In the same pan, sauté chicken in remaining fat until brown on all sides.

I have never written a book that was not born out of a question I needed to answer for myself.

MAY SARTON,
AT SEVENTY,
1984

3. Add onions and mushrooms. Cover and cook slowly until onions are partly tender and beginning to brown. Transfer chicken to a hot platter; pour off all but two or three tablespoons of the fat from the pan.

4. Add shallots and garlic and cook one minute. Blend in flour. Add the wine and cook, stirring constantly, until mixture comes to a boil.

5. Return the chicken to the pan. If the wine does not cover the meat, add water. Tie parsley, bay leaf and thyme in cheesecloth and add to the chicken. Add salt pork or bacon.

6. Simmer on top of the stove or bake, covered, in a 400°F (200°C) oven until the chicken is tender (thirty minutes or longer).

7. Remove herb bag and skim fat from the surface if desired. Arrange chicken, onions and mushrooms on a platter, cover with the sauce and sprinkle with chopped parsley. If carrying as a potluck dish, reheat to bubbling before serving.

Serves 4.

Curried Broccoli & Shrimp Salad

This salad can be prepared quickly in the microwave.

2 cups	fresh broccoli florets	500 mL
1/2 cup	shredded carrots	125 mL
1 small onion, thinly sliced		
1 clove garlic, minced		
2 tbsp	vegetable oil	25 mL
1 tbsp	honey	15 mL
1/2 tsp	curry powder	2 mL
1/4 tsp	caraway seeds	1 mL
pinch salt		
1/8 tsp	cayenne	.5 mL
1 lb	large shrimp, shelled and deveined	500 g
1/3 cup	cocktail peanuts	75 mL

1. In a 2-quart (2-L) casserole, combine broccoli, carrots, onion and garlic.

2. In a small mixing bowl, combine oil, honey, curry powder, caraway seeds, salt and cayenne. Pour over vegetables.

3. Cover and microwave on high for 5 to 6 minutes, or until vegetables are tender crisp, stirring after 3 minutes. Set aside.

4. Place shrimp in a 1 1/2-quart (1.5-L) casserole. Cover and microwave at medium high (70 per cent) for 6 to 12 minutes or until shrimp are opaque, stirring every 2 minutes. Drain.

5. Combine shrimp with vegetables. Re-cover. Chill for 3 to 4 hours, stirring once or twice. Stir in peanuts just before serving.

Serves 4.

Any book which is at all important should be reread immediately.

ARTHUR SCHOPENHAUER

Seafood Casserole

This dish will be a delectable addition to any potluck buffet. If lobster or crab is unavailable, substitute a can of red salmon.

1 cup	chopped onion	250 mL
2 cloves garlic, chopped		
3 cups	chopped celery	750 mL
5 tbsp	butter	75 mL
5 cups	milk	1.25 L
3/4 cup	all-purpose flour	175 mL
1/2 cup	butter	125 mL
1 lb	Cheddar cheese slices	500 g
1 tsp	salt	5 mL
1/4 tsp	pepper	1 mL
1 lb	cooked shrimp	500 g
1 lb	cooked scallops	500 g
1/2 lb	cooked crab	250 g
10 oz	cooked lobster	300 g
5 cups	cooked rice	1.25 L

1. Preheat oven to 350°F (180°C).
2. Sauté onion, garlic and celery in 5 tbsp (75 mL) butter.
3. In a bowl, make a paste with 1/2 cup (125 mL) butter, milk and flour. Add to pan along with all but four slices of cheese and cook gently until cheese is melted. Add salt and pepper.
4. Add shrimp, scallops, crab, lobster and rice. Mix well and transfer to a large casserole. Arrange remaining cheese slices on top.
5. Heat in oven until bubbly and brown, approximately 20 minutes.
6. If carrying as a potluck dish, reheat gently to bubbling.

Serves 6 to 8.

Fiction supplies the only philosophy that many readers know; it establishes their ethical, social and material standards; it confirms them in their prejudices or opens their minds to a wider world.

DOROTHEA BRANDE,
BECOMING A WRITER,
1934

Lemon Charlotte Russe with Raspberry Sauce

A refreshing and elegant dessert.

1 envelope unflavoured gelatin		
1/2 cup	**freshly squeezed lemon juice**	**125 mL**
4 eggs, separated		
1 cup	**granulated sugar**	**250 mL**
1/4 tsp	**salt**	**1 mL**
grated zest of 1 lemon		
16–20 ladyfingers, split		
1 cup	**whipping cream**	**250 mL**
Raspberry Sauce (recipe follows)		

1. In a small bowl, sprinkle gelatin over lemon juice. Let soften for 5 minutes.

2. In the top of a double boiler, combine egg yolks, 1/2 cup (125 mL) sugar and salt. Beat with an electric mixer. Gradually beat in gelatin mixture.

3. Cook over boiling water, stirring constantly, until the mixture begins to thicken and the gelatin is dissolved, about 6 minutes. (Don't let the bottom of the double boiler touch the water.)

4. Pour egg mixture into a large bowl. Add lemon zest. Chill until mixture begins to mound, about 15 to 20 minutes, stirring occasionally.

5. Meanwhile, line the bottom and sides of an 8- or 9-inch (2- or 2.5-L) springform pan with ladyfingers, curved side out.

6. In a large bowl, beat egg whites with an electric mixer until

The test of literature is, I suppose, whether we ourselves live more intensely for the reading of it.

ELIZABETH DREW,
THE MODERN NOVEL,
1926

foamy. Gradually add remaining 1/2 cup (125 mL) sugar and beat until soft peaks form. Whip cream until soft peaks form. Fold beaten egg whites and whipped cream into the lemon-gelatin mixture. Spoon into pan and cover. Chill for 4 hours or overnight.

7. To serve, carefully remove sides of springform pan, and cover top with Raspberry Sauce.

RASPBERRY SAUCE

10 oz pkg. frozen sweetened raspberries, thawed		300 g
1/3 cup	granulated sugar	75 mL
1 tbsp	cornstarch	15 mL

1. Drain raspberries completely, reserving syrup. You should have about 1 1/4 cups (300 mL) of juice. Set drained raspberries aside.

2. Combine sugar and cornstarch in a small saucepan and gradually blend in raspberry juice. Cook over medium heat, stirring constantly, until the mixture thickens, becomes clear, and reaches the boiling point. Reduce heat and simmer for 1 to 2 minutes to completely cook the cornstarch (so as to avoid a starchy taste).

3. Remove from heat and allow to cool. If desired, stir in reserved raspberries.

4. Spread over top of Lemon Charlotte Russe.

Serves 8 to 10.

Fancy cream puffs so soon after breakfast. The very idea made one shudder. All the same, two minutes later Jose and Laura were licking their fingers with that absorbed inward look that only comes from whipped cream.

KATHERINE MANSFIELD,
TITLE STORY,
THE GARDEN PARTY,
1922

Yorkshire Parkin

A pleasant variation on the scone. Traditionally, these treats were put into a wooden parkin box and stored for a week before serving. You can do the same with an airtight tin.

2 1/4 cups	medium oatmeal	550 mL
1 cup	warm milk	250 mL
2 tsp	baking soda	10 mL
1 2/3 cups	wholemeal or plain flour	400 mL
1/2 tsp	salt	2 mL
1–2 tsp	ground ginger	5–10 mL
1 tsp	ground mace	5 mL
1 tsp	ground nutmeg	5 mL
2 tbsp	soft dark brown sugar	25 mL
1/2 cup	molasses (or black treacle)	125 mL
1/2 cup	golden syrup	125 mL
1/4 cup	margarine	50 mL
1 egg, lightly beaten		
1/2 cup	seedless raisins (optional)	125 mL

1. Soak the oatmeal in 3/4 cups (175 mL) of milk for 30 minutes. Dissolve baking soda in remaining milk and set aside.

2. Preheat oven to 325°F (160°C). Grease and line an 8x10-inch (2-L) pan.

3. Sift together flour salt, ginger, mace and nutmeg into a mixing bowl. Stir in sugar.

4. Gently melt molasses or treacle, golden syrup and margarine over a low heat.

The greatest gift is a passion for reading. It is cheap, it consoles, it distracts, it excites, it gives you knowledge of the world and experience of a wide kind. It is a moral illumination.

ELIZABETH HARDWICK, QUOTED IN *THE WRITER'S CHAPBOOK*, ED. GEORGE PLIMPTON, 1989

5. Make a well in the centre of flour mixture. Pour in the syrup mixture, then add the milk-soaked oatmeal.

6. Add the milk with baking soda, the beaten egg and raisins. Mix to form a soft batter and pour into loaf pan.

7. Bake for 40 minutes, or until parkin has an even brown colour and has shrunk slightly away from the sides of the pan.

8. Cool on a wire rack, then cut into squares.

Makes about 50 pieces.

Strawberry Shortcake

This is a wonderful dessert served with or without whipped cream.
Top the shortcake with strawberries, or other seasonal fruit.

4 cups	all-purpose flour	1 L
1 tsp	baking soda	5 mL
2 tbsp	baking powder	25 mL
1 tsp	salt	5 mL
1 cup	shortening	250 mL
2 cups	buttermilk	500 mL
1 cup	granulated sugar	250 mL
1 1/2 pints strawberries	826 mL	
lightly sweetened with 1 tbsp (15 mL) of granulated sugar		

1. Preheat oven to 400°F (200°C). Grease a 12x8-inch (3-L) cake pan.

2. Sift together flour, baking soda, baking powder, and salt in a large mixing bowl. Using a fork or two knives, cut the shortening into the flour mixture until well mixed.

3. Add buttermilk and mix to form dough.

4. Place dough in cake pan and sprinkle sugar on top. Bake for 20 minutes.

5. Cool on a rack and cut into serving pieces. Cover with strawberries and serve with whipped cream if desired.

Serves 12.

≈

... it took me twenty-nine tries to solve the mystery of a fresh strawberry soufflé.

JULIA CHILD

≈

Dundee Cake

This light Scottish fruit cake is delightful when served with tea.
It is best on the day after it is made. The traditional decoration is
blanched split almonds and candied citron.

2 1/2 cups	sifted all-purpose flour	625 mL
1 tsp	baking powder	5 mL
1/2 tsp	salt	2 mL
1 cup	raisins	250 mL
1 cup	currants	250 mL
1/2 cup	chopped candied orange and lemon peel	125 mL
1 cup	butter	250 mL
1 cup	granulated sugar	250 mL
5 eggs		
1/2 cup	ground almonds	125 mL
1 tbsp	orange zest	15 mL
2 tbsp	orange juice	25 mL
1/2 tsp	vanilla	2 mL

1. Preheat oven to 275°F (140°C). Grease a loaf pan, line it with parchment paper, and grease the paper. (A greased and floured tube pan can also be used.)

2. In a bowl, sift together flour, baking powder and salt. Mix in raisins, currants and candied peel.

3. In another bowl, cream butter and sugar well. Beat in eggs one at a time. Add almonds, orange zest, orange juice and vanilla.

4. Stir flour mixture into butter mixture, mixing well. Turn into prepared pan.

5. Bake for 1 to 1 1/4 hours, or until a tester inserted into the centre comes out clean.

Serves 10.

6 / ROBERTSON DAVIES

DAVIES'S CHARACTERS ON FOOD

APPETIZERS

Bread & Butter Pickles

Asparagus-Prosciutto Strudel

Ham Stuffed Eggs

MAIN COURSES

Stuffed Pork Tenderloin

Broccoli Salad

Richmond Tourtière

Chicken Dijon

DESSERTS

Raspberry Supreme Torte

Butter Tarts (version 1)

Butter Tarts (version 2)

Date Squares

CULINARY COMMENTARY

Whether members regard Robertson Davies as a "grand old man of Canadian literature" or an "irrelevant dead white male," his work provides a lively discussion for a reading group. He has created fascinating characters, many of whom arouse strong responses and create page-turner plots in his long fiction. Davies's settings are equally distinctive, involving a particular early-twentieth-century southern-Ontario social milieu centred on an anglophile Toronto. Since he was so prolific in several genres over such a long period of time, attitudes and style changes also make for interesting consideration.

Many of the sidebars for this chapter present a small selection of the witty comments on food and writing to be found in Davies's work. Below is a selected list of his fiction.

THE SALTERTON TRILOGY
   Tempest-Tost, 1951
   Leaven of Malice, 1954
   A Mixture of Frailties, 1958

THE DEPTFORD TRILOGY
   Fifth Business, 1970
   The Manticore, 1972
   World of Wonders, 1975

THE CORNISH TRILOGY
   The Rebel Angels, 1981
   What's Bred in the Bone, 1985
   The Lyre of Orpheus, 1988

THE TORONTO BOOKS
   Murther and Walking Spirits, 1991
   The Cunning Man, 1994

Bread and Butter Pickles

A jar of this reliable rendition of an old favourite, along with a piece of old Cheddar, makes a quick appetizer. The hostess or host gets to keep leftovers.

4 lbs	unwaxed cucumbers	2 kg
1/2 lb	onions	250 g
1/2 cup	coarse salt	125 mL
2 1/2 cups	granulated sugar	625 mL
1 1/2 tsp	celery seed	7 mL
1 1/2 tsp	mustard seed	7 mL
1 1/2 tsp	turmeric	7 mL
2 1/2 cups	cider vinegar	625 mL

1. Remove the tops and tails from the cucumbers and cut into 1/8-inch (2-mm) slices. Peel the onions and cut into 1/8-inch (2-mm) slices.

2. Layer cucumbers and onions with salt in a large glass or stainless steel bowl. (Do not use aluminium.) Cover with cold water; cover the bowl and refrigerate for 4 to 5 hours or overnight.

3. Wash four 1-pint (500-mL) jars in hot soapy water, place in canner, cover with water and bring to a boil. Hold at boiling point for at least 10 minutes. Place lids (use only new ones) in the canner for the last 5 minutes.

4. Drain, rinse and drain vegetables again. Refrigerate in a colander set in the bowl while you prepare the sugar, spices and vinegar mixture.

5. Combine sugar, celery seed, mustard seed, turmeric and

Royalty was supping in an inner room with a few personal friends, but something of their magic lingered in the large supper-room, where Marie-Louise exclaimed over BLANCHAILLES À LA DIABLE, POULARDS À LA NORVÉGIENNE, JAMBONS D'ESPAGNE À LA BASQUE, ORTOLANS RÔTIS SUR CANAPÉS, *and ate them all, following with a great many patisseries and two ices.*

WHAT'S BRED
IN THE BONE,
1985

vinegar in a 6-to-8 quart (6-to-8 L) pan. Heat to a boil, stirring to dissolve sugar. When mixture boils, add vegetables all at once. Stir to encourage even heating, and heat just to the boiling point. Adjust heat to keep mixture hot, but not boiling.

6. Using a slotted spoon, remove vegetables from mixture and transfer to the hot jars, filling each to within 1 inch (2.5 cm) of the top. Pour boiling mixture from pan into jars. Using a tea strainer or a fine sieve, remove remaining spices from the pan and divide among the jars. Leave 1/4 inch (1 cm) of space at the top of each jar. (Discard any remaining mixture.) Wipe the rims and centre the lids. Screw lids to fingertip tight.

7. Process jars in boiling water bath for 10 minutes.

8. Leave jars to cool for 24 hours. Store in cool, dark place for at least a month before using.

Makes 4 pints (500 mL).

Asparagus-Prosciutto Strudel

An elegant presentation of extra-special ingredients. The number of prosciutto slices needed will vary according to the size of the slices. Serve the strudel either at room temperature or warm slightly in a 200°F (95°C) oven.

1 lb	asparagus, washed well, bottom tips removed	500 g
4 oz	light cream cheese	125 g
6 oz	goat cheese or grated Fontina cheese	170 g
1 egg		
2 tbsp	minced fresh parsley	25 mL
2 tbsp	minced fresh chives	25 mL
1 tsp	dried tarragon	5 mL
pepper (to taste)		
6–8 slices thinly sliced prosciutto		
8 sheets phyllo dough		
1/4 cup	oil or melted butter	50 mL

1. Preheat oven to 400°F (200°C). Grease a baking sheet.
2. Steam asparagus until slightly crunchy. Cool under running water. Set aside.
3. Cream together cream cheese, goat cheese, egg and herbs.
4. Layer 4 sheets of phyllo, brushing each sheet with oil or melted butter. On the short side of the top sheet of phyllo, place 3 or 4 pieces of prosciutto in a single layer. Spread half the cheese mixture on top of the prosciutto. Lay half of the asparagus spears on top of the cheese mixture. Tuck in the sides

We'll top off with lots and lots of cheese; the goatiest and messiest you have, because I like my cheese opinionated.

THE REBEL ANGELS,
1981

125

and bottom of the phyllo and fold over once. Place strudel on baking sheet and brush with oil.

5. Repeat step 4 with the remaining phyllo, prosciutto, cheese mixture and asparagus.

6. Bake strudels for approximately 20 to 25 minutes.

7. Let cool 10 minutes, then cut into serving pieces. If carrying as a potluck dish, cut immediately before serving.

Serves 8.

Ham Stuffed Eggs

For a tasty variation of this delicious appetizer, place the stuffed eggs in a shallow, greased casserole, brush with melted butter, dust with paprika, and bake at 350–375°F (180–190°C) for 5 to 10 minutes.

6 hard-boiled eggs		
1/3 cup	minced cooked ham	75 mL
1 tsp	dry mustard	5 mL
1/2 tsp	salt	2 mL
1/4 tsp	ground black pepper	1 mL
3–4 tbsp	sour cream	45–60 mL
sprigs of parsley (for garnish)		

1. Cut eggs in half lengthwise. Remove the yolks and mash with a fork in a bowl. Add ham, mustard, salt, pepper and sour cream. Mix well until combined. If necessary, add a little more sour cream.
2. Fill egg whites with the ham mixture and garnish with sprigs of parsley.

Serves 6.

A good meal should be like a performance; the Edwardians understood that. Their meals were a splendid form of theatre, like a play by Pinero, with skilful preparation, expectation, denouement, and satisfactory ending. The well-made play; the well-made meal. Drama one can eat.

THE REBEL ANGELS,
1981

Stuffed Pork Tenderloin

The fruit in this stuffing adds an interesting flavour and texture.

1 lb	pork tenderloin (2 whole)	500 g
2 tbsp	butter	25 mL
1/4 cup	finely chopped onion	50 mL
1/4 cup	finely chopped celery	50 mL
1/2 cup	chopped apple	125 mL
2 tbsp	raisins	25 mL
1/2 tsp	salt	2 mL
pepper (to taste)		
1/2 tsp	summer savory	2 mL
2 cups	soft bread crumbs	500 mL
4 slices bacon		

1. Preheat oven to 325°F (160°C).
2. Split tenderloins lengthwise, without cutting through to bottom, and flatten with a mallet.
3. In large skillet, melt butter. Sauté onion and celery until soft. Stir in chopped apple, raisins, salt, pepper, savory and bread crumbs.
4. Cover one tenderloin with stuffing. Lay the other tenderloin on top and wrap bacon slices around outside. Secure with string or toothpicks.
5. Place on rack in roasting pan. Bake for about 50 minutes or until meat is nicely browned and the juices run clear when the tenderloin is pierced with a fork.

Serves 4.

Broccoli Salad

This recipe can be easily expanded to feed a crowd. Make the dressing the day before and chill it overnight so that the raisins plump up and the flavours blend nicely.

1 1/2 cups	mayonnaise	375 mL
2 tbsp	red wine vinegar	25 mL
1 tbsp	Dijon mustard	15 mL
3 tbsp	honey	45 mL
1/2 cup	raisins	125 mL
2 bunches of broccoli, stems removed		
1 red onion, finely chopped		
1 cup	sunflower seeds or pine nuts, lightly roasted	250 mL
2-6 slices of bacon, cooked and crumbled		

1. Blend together mayonnaise, vinegar, mustard, honey and raisins to make the dressing. Chill overnight.
2. Just before serving, break broccoli florets into small pieces. Combine broccoli, onion, sunflower seeds and bacon. Lightly coat with dressing.

Serves 6 to 8.

They all ate bowls of rindze *and* pixtia, *which was tripe seethed in pig's foot jelly, and not as bad as it sounds. Darcourt showed great appetite, as was expected; those who consult oracles must not be choosy. The dish was followed by something heavy and cheesy called saviako. Darcout thanked God for a strong shot of Yerko's home-made plum brandy, which was stupefying to the palate, but burned a hole through the heavy mixture in the stomach.*

THE LYRE OF ORPHEUS, 1988

Richmond Tourtière

Nothing in Canadian cuisine is more idiosyncratic than tourtière. If it isn't your mother's recipe, it isn't right! This tourtière can be frozen after it is baked. To serve, warm it in a 375°F (190°C) oven for 30 to 35 minutes.

1 lb	ground meat (2 parts beef to 1 part pork)	500 g
1/2 cup	potato water	125 mL
1 medium onion, chopped		
1 clove garlic (or to taste), minced		
1/2 tsp	salt	2 mL
1/2 tsp	thyme	2 mL
1 1/2 tsp	sage	7 mL
1/4 tsp	dry mustard	1 mL
1/8 tsp	cloves	.5 mL
1 medium potato, cooked and mashed		
pastry for a double-crust pie		

1. Preheat oven to 450°F (230°C).
2. Combine meat, potato water, onion, garlic, salt, thyme, sage, mustard and cloves in a medium-sized pot. Cook on high until the meat is browned, breaking up lumps with a spoon. Simmer at medium-low until all the liquid is absorbed.
3. Remove from heat, add mashed potato, and chill.
4. When chilled, place meat mixture in unbaked pie shell, cover with second sheet of pastry. Press the edges together firmly. Cut decorative steam holes in the upper crust.
5. Bake for 10 minutes. Lower heat to 350°F (180°C) and bake for 20 minutes or until completely cooked.

Serves 10.

Chicken Dijon

This recipe can be prepared ahead of time and served either hot or cold.

6 chicken breasts		
salt and freshly ground pepper (to taste)		
1/4 cup	**Dijon mustard**	**50 mL**
1/3 cup	**plain yogurt or sour cream**	**75 mL**
1/2 cup	**fresh bread crumbs**	**125 mL**
1 tsp	**thyme**	**5 mL**
salt and pepper (to taste)		

1. Preheat oven to 350°F (180°C). Lightly grease a baking sheet.
2. Remove skin from chicken and sprinkle lightly with salt and pepper.
3. In a small bowl, mix mustard, yogurt and thyme. In another bowl, combine bread crumbs, salt and pepper.
4. Spread each piece of chicken with mustard mixture, then roll in bread crumb mixture. Place on baking sheet.
5. Bake for 45 to 50 minutes for bone-in breasts, or 30 to 35 minutes for boneless breasts.
6. If carrying as a potluck dish, reheat briefly in the microwave.

Serves 6 as main dish, or 12 as smaller buffet portions.

Our Sundays have become quite a Toronto institution without our ever having done much about it ... We both work like stink from Friday through Sat., preparing the goodies, which I must say are pretty lavish — scones with jam and whipped cream are a popular item and cucumber sandwiches by the hod.

THE CUNNING MAN, 1994

Raspberry Supreme Torte

This dessert is stunning to look at and delicious to eat. If you are in a hurry, buy ready-made meringue nests at the supermarket instead of making them. If you want to avoid the seeds, squeeze all the juice from the berries through a sieve and add to the syrup.

Preheat oven to 250°F (120°C). Cover two cookie sheets with parchment paper.

MERINGUES

4 egg whites		
1/4 tsp	cream of tartar	1 mL
1/4 tsp	salt	1 mL
1 cup	granulated sugar	250 mL
1/2 tsp	almond extract	2 mL

1. To make meringues, beat egg whites, cream of tartar and salt until soft peaks form. Gradually add sugar and almond extract, beating until stiff peaks form.

2. Smooth half of the meringue into a large round shape about 1/2-inch (1-cm) thick on parchment paper or one of the cookie sheets. Do the same with the remaining meringue on the second cookie sheet. The two rounds should be equal in size.

3. Bake for 1 1/2 hours or until completely dry. Lift meringues from parchment paper and cool on wire racks.

TORTE

2 cups	whipping cream	500 mL
1/4 cup	icing sugar	50 mL
2 tbsp	orange liqueur	25 mL

1. In a large bowl, whip cream and icing sugar until stiff. Beat in liqueur.
2. Break meringues into bite-sized pieces and fold into whipped cream.
3. Pack the mixture into a lightly-greased 9-inch (2-5 L) springform pan. Cover with foil and freeze.

SAUCE

10 oz pkg. frozen sweetened raspberries, thawed	300 g
1/3 cup granulated sugar	75 mL
1 tbsp cornstarch	15 mL
sweetened whipped cream (for garnish)	

1. Drain raspberries completely, reserving juice. You should have about 1 1/4 cups (300 mL) of juice. Set drained raspberries aside.
2. Combine sugar and cornstarch in a small saucepan and gradually blend in raspberry juice. Cook over medium heat, stirring constantly, until the mixture thickens, becomes clear and reaches the boiling point. Reduce heat and simmer for 1 to 2 minutes to completely cook the cornstarch (so as to avoid a starchy taste).
3. Remove from heat and cool. If desired, stir in drained raspberries.

Fifteen minutes before serving, remove the torte from the freezer. Remove sides of pan. Drizzle top with raspberry sauce and garnish with additional whipped cream if desired. Serve with remaining raspberry sauce.

Serves 8 to 10.

The gentle art of gastronomy is a friendly one. It hurdles the language barrier, makes friends among civilized people, and warms the heart.

SAMUEL CHAMBERLAIN

133

Butter Tarts

(VERSION 1)

This is Elizabeth's version of a classic Canadian treat. For the tart shells, she recommends a shortening pastry. The filling can be made two days in advance, covered and stored in the refrigerator.

24 medium-sized tart shells, unbaked		
1/4 cup	raisins or currants	50 mL
1/3 cup	walnut pieces	75 mL
1 cup	corn syrup	250 mL
2/3 cup	brown sugar, packed	150 mL
1/4 cup	salted butter	50 mL
2 tsp	vanilla	10 mL
2 eggs, beaten		

1. Preheat oven to 425°F (220°C).
2. Place a few raisins and walnuts in each tart shell. (Elizabeth likes three or four of each.)
3. Combine butter and sugar in a saucepan, and heat to dissolve sugar. Add corn syrup and heat to boiling.
4. Cool the mixture to warm. Add beaten eggs and vanilla.
5. Pour filling into tart shells.
6. Bake at 425°F (220°C) for 10 minutes. Reduce heat to 375°F (190°C) and bake for 5 to 7 minutes, watching carefully to make sure the tarts do not burn.
7. Remove from oven. Loosen the tarts while they are hot so they can be removed easily after the pans cool.

Makes 24 medium tarts.

Butter Tarts

(VERSION 2)

Here is C-J's version of the same Canadian classic. C-J prefers using a lard pastry for her tart shells. Ready-made tart shells can also be used.

24 small tart shells, unbaked		
2/3 cup	butter	150 mL
1 cup	brown sugar	250 mL
2/3 cup	dark corn syrup	150 mL
2 large eggs, beaten		
2 tsp	vanilla	10 mL
1 cup	chopped raisins	250 mL
1 cup	chopped and toasted pecans	250 mL

1. Preheat oven to 400°F (200°C).
2. Melt butter in a small saucepan. Add brown sugar and corn syrup, and heat slowly over low temperature until sugar is melted. Cool completely.
3. Add beaten eggs, vanilla, raisins and pecans and mix well.
4. Fill tart shells about half full.
5. Bake on low shelf of oven for 12 to 15 minutes.

Makes 24 small but tasty tarts.

The splendour of the meal quite overcame any lingering coldness she, as a French Canadian, might feel about British royalty. They knew what food was, these people! As she ate, and under the influence of an 1837 sherry, an 1892 champagne, and 1874 Château Langoa, ... he confided to the Major more than once that his Sovereign really knew how to do things properly.

WHAT'S BRED
IN THE BONE,
1985

Date Squares

There are a number of possible variations for this standard classic. For example, you might add chopped nuts to the date mixture. The mixture can be used as a filler between two oatmeal cookies and is also a delicious filling for a chocolate cake (with the addition of a little grated orange zest and orange juice).

1 lb	dates	500 mL
1 cup	water	250 mL
1/2 cup	granulated sugar	125 mL
1 1/2 cups	rolled oats	375 mL
1 1/2 cups	all-purpose flour	375 mL
1 tsp	baking powder	5 mL
1/4 tsp	salt	1 mL
1/2–1 cup	brown sugar	125–250 mL
1 cup	butter	250 mL
1/4 cup	walnuts	50 mL

1. Preheat oven to 350°F (180°C).
2. Cut dates into small pieces and place in saucepan. Add water and granulated sugar. Cook until the mixture is quite thick, stirring often to prevent scorching. Allow to cool.
3. In a bowl, combine oats, flour, baking powder, salt and brown sugar. Cut in butter until the mixture resembles coarse crumbs. Add walnuts and mix.
4. Press half the crumb mixture into a 9-inch (2.5-L) square pan. Cover with date mixture, and sprinkle remaining crumb mixture on top.
5. Bake for 45 minutes. Cool, and cut into squares.

Makes 18 squares.

Section Three

ORGANIZING
BOOK CLUB MEETINGS
BY GENRE

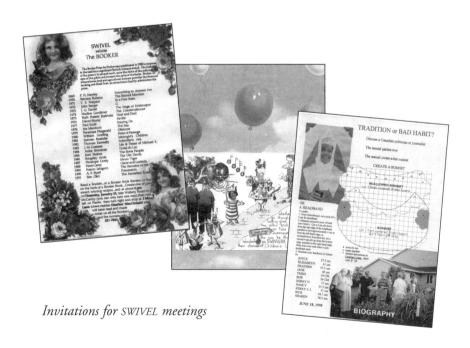

Invitations for SWIVEL meetings

7 / LITERARY AWARD WINNERS

LA CRÈME DE LA CRÈME

APPETIZERS

Asparagus & Prosciutto

Chicken Slice

Brie with Mango Chutney & Pecans

Pigs in Blankets

MAIN COURSES

Meat Loaf en Croûte

Artichoke Florentine

Ham & Caulifower Supper Dish

Avocado & Grapefruit Salad

with Poppy Seed Dressing

DESSERTS

Raspberry Trifle

Damson Plum Pie

Double Chocolate Bombe

Nanaimo Bars

THE PICK OF THE CROP

On several occasions, SWIVEL has organized meetings around the winners of major literary awards. We discovered or heard summaries of wonderful choices and were also introduced to and inspired to read exceptional new works. Several of these selections were chosen as titles to be read by the whole group in the following year. Folks who had never read a mystery were introduced to the genre through the Edgars. New poetry readers were surprised to discover the pleasure of "eating a poem" just before bedtime, and reading aloud favourite poems (or selected passages) has added to the delight of a number of club evenings.

Meetings of this type can be based on major book prizes such as the Giller, the Booker and the Governor-General's Literary Awards. However, there are many more prestigious Canadian literary awards — a number of which are described in the sidebars of this chapter — and a wide variety of genre awards for forms such as poetry or mystery. Members can be invited to choose a winner to read and report on.

The short lists for literary awards can provide worthwhile shopping lists for reading material between meeting dates. Meetings might also be organized around the short list, with members choosing one or more titles to read before the winner of the award is announced.

THE INTREPID SURFER

A visit to http://www.literature-awards.com provides a link to many literary awards, from A to Z.

Asparagus & Prosciutto

This appetizer is simple but delicious, especially when local asparagus is in season. The prosciutto slices should be thick and large enough to roll easily. If prosciutto is not available, substitute Westphalian ham. You can use plain cream cheese, but the dill and fines herbes *varieties are also tasty.*

8–12 asparagus spears (slender to medium thickness)		
4 oz	**cream cheese**	**125 g**
4–6 thin slices of prosciutto		

1. Preheat oven to 400°F (200°C).
2. Wash asparagus, break off ends and blanch in boiling water for 2 minutes. Drain and rinse in cold water.
3. Spread cream cheese on prosciutto and lay 2 spears of asparagus on each slice. Roll up and fasten with a toothpick. Place on a baking sheet.
4. Bake for 3 to 4 minutes.

Serves 4 to 6.

Chicken Slice

Another quick, original appetizer. Party bread is smaller and more square than regular loaves.

2 chicken breasts, cooked		
1 cup	mayonnaise	250 mL
4.5 oz can	green chilies, drained and chopped	127 mL
3/4 cup	grated sharp Cheddar cheese	175 mL
1/4 cup	finely chopped onions	50 mL
1 loaf party bread, sliced		

1. Cut chicken into small pieces. Combine chicken, mayonnaise, chilies, cheese and onions. Spread mixture on bread slices and arrange on cookie sheet.
2. Broil 5 minutes or until lightly browned. Serve hot.

Serves 6 to 8.

Brie with Mango Chutney & Pecans

This elegant appetizer is easy to assemble at the last minute. You can use any type of sweet chutney and, if desired, substitute hazelnuts for the pecans. Serve with Melba toast or whole wheat crackers, and place a serving knife beside the plate so that guests don't break their crackers while trying to spread the cheese.

8 oz round ripe brie cheese		250 g
1/4 cup	mango chutney	50 mL
1/2 cup	whole pecans	125 mL

1. Preheat oven to 325°F (160°C).
2. Slice top rind off brie and discard.
3. Spread the mango chutney over exposed cheese and cover with pecans.
4. Bake for 10 to 12 minutes, or until the cheese is slightly runny.

Serves 4 to 6.

Pigs in Blankets

*These appetizers are guaranteed to provide almost instant pleasure.
Serve them with chili sauce. They can be made ahead of time and frozen.
Varying the types of sausages and mustards makes a nice surprise.*

12 oz	frozen puff pastry	395 g
1 lb	sausages	500 g
2 tbsp	mustard	25 mL
1 egg, beaten		

1. Preheat oven to 400°F (200°C).
2. Thaw puff pastry according to package directions (minimum time is 2 hours). Cut into strips.
3. Prick sausages with a fork. Cook in enough water to cover for 5–7 minutes, or until juices no longer run when sausages are pierced with a fork. Drain.
4. Spread pastry strips with mustard and roll a sausage in each one. Brush rolls with egg and place on cookie sheet.
5. Bake until browned, about 15 minutes.
6. Cool slightly and slice rolls into 1-inch (2-cm) pieces. (Rolls can also be frozen whole and sliced after they are removed from the freezer.)

Makes 16 pieces.

Meat Loaf en Croûte

A traditional dish brought to you from eighteenth-century Louisbourg.

FILLING

1 1/4 lb	finely chopped beef	625 g
1/2 lb	finely chopped ham	250 g
1/2 lb	finely chopped pork	250 g
1/2 cup	minced fresh parsley (or 2 tbsp / 25 mL dried)	125 mL
1/4 cup	minced green onion	50 mL
1 onion, minced		
3 shallots, minced		
1 or 2 cloves garlic, minced		
2 tsp	salt (or to taste)	10 mL
1/4 tsp	pepper (or to taste)	1 mL

PASTRY WRAP

2 cups	all-purpose flour	500 mL
about 1/2 cup	water	about 125 mL

1. Preheat oven to 300°F (150°C).

2. Combine all filling ingredients in a bowl and mix thoroughly. Shape into a ball.

3. To make pastry wrap, combine flour and water. Use just enough water to make a soft but not sticky dough.

4. Roll out dough to about 1/8 inch (.5 cm) thickness. Wrap around the ball of meat and wet the edges with water or egg white. Press firmly to seal.

5. Bake for 3 1/2 hours. Remove from oven and cool completely (overnight is best). Cut into thin slices. Serve cold.

Serves 8 to 10.

Artichoke Florentine

A stylish entrée.

16 artichoke bottoms (canned)		
2 cups	**frozen spinach, thawed**	**500 mL**
2 tbsp	**butter**	**25 mL**
2 tbsp	**all-purpose flour**	**25 mL**
1/2 cup	**chicken broth**	**125 mL**
1/2 cup	**light cream**	**125 mL**
salt and pepper (to taste)		
freshly grated nutmeg (to taste)		
1/2 cup	**grated Gruyère cheese**	**125 mL**

1. Preheat oven to 350°F (180°C). Butter a shallow baking dish.

2. Place artichoke bottoms side by side in baking dish.

3. Drain spinach and chop finely. Set aside.

4. In a saucepan, blend butter and flour and cook over low heat. Add chicken broth and bring to a boil. Stir until thickened. Remove from heat and stir in cream. Season with salt, pepper and freshly grated nutmeg.

5. Mix spinach into cream sauce. Pour over artichoke bottoms. Sprinkle cheese on top.

6. Bake uncovered for 30 minutes.

7. If carrying as a potluck dish, reheat briefly in microwave.

Serves 8.

Ham & Cauliflower Supper Dish

A quick, comforting winter dish. For extra flavour, use smoked ham.

1/2 medium cauliflower		
2 tbsp	margarine or butter	25 mL
2 tbsp	all-purpose flour	25 mL
1 cup	milk	250 mL
1/2 cup	grated Cheddar or mozzarella cheese	125 mL
2 tbsp	fresh coriander and parsley	25 mL
1 cup	diced cooked ham	250 mL
1/2 cup	diced sweet red or yellow pepper	125 mL
salt and freshly ground pepper (to taste)		
1/4 cup	fresh bread crumbs	50 mL
1/4 cup	Parmesan cheese	50 mL

1. Preheat oven to 375°F (190°C). Lightly grease an 8-inch (2-L) baking dish.

2. Break cauliflower into small florets and blanch in boiling water until tender but still firm. Drain and set aside.

3. In a saucepan over medium heat, melt margarine or butter. Add flour and stir until smooth. Pour in milk and stir until slightly thickened. Add Cheddar cheese, coriander, parsley, salt and pepper. Stir until cheese is melted. (Keep the sauce thick at this stage as it tends to thin during baking.)

4. Add cauliflower, ham and pepper to the sauce and stir gently. Pour into baking dish.

5. Combine bread crumbs and Parmesan cheese and sprinkle over the casserole.

6. Bake for 30 minutes or until heated through and brown on top.

7. If carrying as a potluck dish, reheat briefly in a microwave oven.

Serves 6.

Avocado & Grapefruit Salad with Poppy Seed Dressing

This salad is refreshingly different and lovely to look at as well as to eat.

2 heads Boston lettuce
1 large pink grapefruit
2 avocados, slightly soft to the touch
3 or 4 slices red onion
Poppy Seed Dressing (recipe follows)

1. Tear lettuce into bite sized-pieces, wash thoroughly, drain and chill.
2. Peel and section grapefruit.
3. Peel and slice avocado. Rub each slice with lemon to prevent browning.
4. Separate red onion slices into rings.
5. Combine lettuce, grapefruit, avocado and onion in a large salad bowl. Toss with a liberal amount of Poppy Seed Dressing.

Serves 4.

POPPY SEED DRESSING

1/3 cup	honey	75 mL
1 tsp	salt	5 mL
2 tbsp	vinegar	25 mL
1 tbsp	prepared mustard	15 mL
3/4 cup	salad oil	175 mL
1 tbsp	finely chopped onion	15 mL
2–3 tsp	poppy seed	10–15 mL

1. In a small jar, blend honey, salt, vinegar and mustard.
2. Gradually add oil, stirring to blend thoroughly. Stir in onion and poppy seed, and shake vigorously.
3. Cover and chill for several hours to blend flavours. Shake well again before using.

Makes about 1 1/4 cups (300 mL).

Raspberry Trifle

This recipe is an exceptional rendition of an old favourite. You'll want to prepare the White Chocolate Custard ahead of the cake. When preparing the cake, you can substitute a raspberry liqueur for the orange juice or use a mixture of juice and liqueur. To make a wonderful summer trifle use 1 1/2 pints (750 mL) of fresh berries and 2/3 cups (150 mL) of sugar to replace the frozen berries.

WHITE CHOCOLATE CUSTARD

1 tbsp	unflavoured gelatin	15 mL
1/2 cup	water	125 mL
3 eggs, separated		
1/2 cup	granulated sugar	125 mL
2 tsp	cornstarch	10 mL
1 cup	milk	250 mL
6 oz	white chocolate, melted	170 g
pinch nutmeg		
1 tsp	orange zest	5 mL
1 tbsp	granulated sugar	15 mL
1/2 cup	whipping cream	125 mL

1. Soften gelatin in water as directed on package and set aside.

2. In a bowl, combine egg yolks, 1/2 cup (125 mL) sugar and cornstarch and beat until smooth.

3. Heat milk in small saucepan, then gradually add milk to egg mixture. Return custard to saucepan and continue cooking until slightly thickened.

4. Remove custard from heat. Stir in chocolate, nutmeg, orange zest and gelatin. Cool to room temperature.

5. Beat egg whites with 1 tbsp (15 mL) sugar until stiff. Fold into custard. Chill until partially set.

6. Whip cream until stiff and fold into custard.

CAKE

12 oz	pound cake	375 g
12 oz jar	raspberry jam	375 g
1/2 cup	orange juice or raspberry liqueur	125 mL
	(or a mix of both)	
4 pkgs (10 oz / 300 g) frozen raspberries, thawed and drained		

TOPPING

1 1/2 cups	whipping cream	375 mL
2 tbsp	granulated sugar	25 mL
2 oz	bittersweet chocolate (for garnish)	60 g
2 oz	white chocolate (for garnish)	60 g
1/4 cup	toasted almond slivers (for garnish)	50 mL

1. Cut pound cake into two layers, then slice horizontally into 1/2-inch (1-cm) slices. Spread half the slices with raspberry jam and cover with the remaining slices to form sandwiches. Cut the sandwiches into thin fingers (or cubes if you prefer).

2. Line the bottom of a glass trifle dish with half the fingers. Cover with half the remaining raspberry jam and sprinkle with half the orange juice. Spoon half the White Chocolate Custard over cake fingers and top with half the raspberries.

3. Repeat layers with remaining cake fingers, jam, orange juice, custard and raspberries. Cover and chill for several hours.

4. Just before serving, prepare the topping. Add the sugar to the whipping cream and whip until soft peaks form. Shave white and dark chocolate. Garnish trifle with whipped cream, chocolate shavings and almonds.

Serves 10.

Damson Plum Pie

Tart sweet plums and a light custard — if desired, substitute gooseberry jam for the damson plum jam. Serve with whipped cream.

3 eggs		
1 cup	damson plum jam	250 mL
1/4 cup	melted butter	50 mL
2 tbsp	sherry	25 mL
1 9-inch (23-cm) pie shell, unbaked		

1. Preheat oven to 400°F (200°C).
2. Beat eggs until thick. Beat in the jam. Stir in butter and sherry. Turn into pie shell.
3. Bake for about 10 minutes. Reduce heat to 300°F (150°C) and continue baking for about 25 minutes.

Serves 8.

Double Chocolate Bombe

This rich dessert is worth all the effort. Make it the day before you want to serve it.

1 oz	semi-sweet chocolate (1 square)	30 g

WHITE MOUSSE

1 tsp	unflavoured gelatin	5 mL
2/3 cup	whipping cream	150 mL
6 oz	white chocolate	170 g
2 tbsp	butter	25 mL
2 eggs, separated		
1/4 cup	granulated sugar	50 mL

DARK MOUSSE

1/3 cup	whipping cream	75 mL
5 oz	semi-sweet chocolate	150 g
2 tbsp	butter	25 mL
2 eggs, separated		
1/4 cup	granulated sugar	50 mL

1. Melt square of semi-sweet chocolate. Line a 6-cup mixing bowl with plastic wrap and drizzle inner surface with melted chocolate. Freeze.

2. Make the white mousse. Pour cream into a small saucepan and sprinkle the gelatin on top. Let stand 5 minutes to soften.

3. Bring cream to a boil and remove from heat. Add white chocolate and butter and stir until melted. Blend in egg yolks until thick and blend into chocolate mixture.

4. Beat egg whites until frothy. Gradually add sugar and continue beating until stiff peaks form. Fold into chocolate mixture. Pour into the chocolate-coated bowl and freeze for 30 minutes.

5. To make the dark mousse, follow the procedure described in steps 3 and 4 (omit the gelatin step). Pour on top of the white mousse.

6. Freeze until set, at least 8 hours.

7. To serve, unmould onto serving plate and remove plastic wrap.

Serves 6.

Oddly, I felt no pressure at all after winning the Pulitzer. ... I've never believed that writers must "top" themselves with each new book ... Most of us write out of where we are at the moment and we write the very best book we're capable of.

CAROL SHIELDS,
IN AN INTERVIEW ON WINNING THE
PULITZER PRIZE FOR
THE STONE DIARIES,
1995

Nanaimo Bars

BARS

1/2 cup	butter, softened	125 mL
1/4 cup	granulated sugar	50 mL
5 tbsp	cocoa	75 mL
1 tsp	vanilla	5 mL
2 eggs, beaten		
2 cups	graham cracker crumbs	500 mL
1 cup	coconut	250 mL
1/2 cup	walnuts	125 mL

FROSTING

1/4 cup	butter	50 mL
3 tbsp	milk	45 mL
2 tbsp	vanilla custard powder	25 mL
2 cups	sifted icing sugar	500 mL
4 oz	semi-sweet chocolate	125 g
1 tbsp	butter	15 mL

1. Grease a 9-inch (2.5 L) square pan.
2. To make the bars, combine butter, sugar, cocoa, vanilla and eggs in a microwave-safe dish and mix well. Microwave on high until the mixture resembles a custard.
3. Combine crumbs, coconut and walnuts in a bowl. Add cocoa mixture and stir to blend. Pack into pan.
4. To make the frosting, mix butter, milk and custard powder in a bowl. Blend in icing sugar. Spread over cocoa-crumb mixture in pan. Allow to stand for 15 minutes or until hardened.
5. In a small saucepan, melt chocolate and butter together. Spread over frosting. Allow to set. Cut into bars in pan and serve.

Makes 30 bars.

8 / CHILDREN'S LITERATURE

AWARD-WINNING SELECTIONS TO APPEAL TO THE CHILD IN EACH OF US

APPETIZERS

Pickle Puffs

Cheese Biscuits

MAIN COURSES

Country Meat Loaf

24-Hour Coleslaw

Shepherd's Pie

Lemon Apple Salad

Creamy Cheese Pasta

Turkey Chili

DESSERTS

Lemon Snow

Apple Upside-Down Cake

NOURISHING CREATIVITY

No book is really worth reading at the age of ten which is not equally (and often far more) worth reading at the age of fifty and beyond.

C.S. LEWIS

Our experience at SWIVEL certainly supports Lewis's comment. We have had two evenings devoted to children's literature. The first was entitled "Classics Missed as a Child." For the second, members chose to read either a children's book or a book about children's literature. Discussing the best-loved books from our past as well as our new discoveries led to a sharing of personal reminiscences and a broader examination of social and cultural history.

Indeed, discussion about treasured childhood books seems to encourage comfortable and open interaction among club members. Perhaps (as the social psychologists tell us) it is good to let our "inner child" emerge. After all, it is rather difficult to remain completely serious while mounting a staunch defense of *Reddy Fox* against *Stuart Little* or the Hardy Boys against Nancy Drew. High-flown arguments are quite likely to dissolve into gales of laughter.

Discussions of children's literature can also focus on current bestsellers and provide useful information for buying gifts. When shared with children or grandchildren, the joy of a good book can bring a special kind of closeness. Don't be fooled into thinking that children's literature is a lesser form of adult literature. Children's books can be remarkably engaging, well-written and intriguingly illustrated.

Reading lists of children's books are readily available — ask your local librarian or bookseller. CBC Radio also features discussions of children's books, particularly around the holiday season. The sidebars in this chapter present a selection of Canadian and international awards for children's books with lists of recent winners.

INTREPID SURFER

If for no other reason than the sheer joy of it, have a look at The Peter Rabbitt™ Official Web site (www.peterrabbit.co.uk). You'll probably want to share it with the next adult you meet. Another site that is fun for children and informative for parents is CBC's www.cbc4kids.ca. The Canadian Children's Book Centre site (www.bookcentre.ca) is up-to-date and inclusive.

1996
PAUL YEE,
Ghost Train

∽

BEST ILLUSTRATION

2001
MIREILLE LEVERT,
An Island in the Soup

2000
MARIE-LOUISE GAY,
Yuck, A Love Story

1999
GARY CLEMENT,
The Great Poochini

1998
KADY MACDONALD DENTON,
A Child's Treasury of Nursery Rhymes

1997
BARBARA REID,
The Party

1996
ERIC BEDDOWS,
The Rooster's Gift

∽

Pickle Puffs

What a nice thing to do to a pickle. If desired, you can substitute twenty-four medium stuffed olives for the pickles. The puffs will keep for about a week.

6 sweet gherkin pickles, drained		
1 cup	grated extra old Cheddar cheese	250 mL
1/4 cup	butter	50 mL
1/2 cup	all-purpose flour	125 mL
1/2 tsp	paprika	2 mL

1. Preheat oven to 400°F (200°C).
2. Dry pickles and cut each one into four pieces.
3. Blend cheese with butter. Stir in flour, paprika and mix well.
4. Form dough into 24 small balls with a piece of pickle in the centre of each.
5. Bake for 12 minutes. Watch carefully as the puffs will brown quickly.
6. Cool and store in an airtight container.

Makes 24 puffs.

Cheese Biscuits

These thin, crispy, bite-sized biscuits make tasty starters for a potluck meal.

1/2 cup	butter	125 mL
2 cups	grated old Cheddar cheese	500 mL
1/2 cup	grated Parmesan cheese	125 mL
1 cup	all-purpose flour	250 mL
1/4 tsp	cayenne pepper	1 mL
1/2 tsp	salt	2 mL
1 egg, beaten		
1/2 cup	finely chopped nuts	125 mL

1. Preheat oven to 375°F (190°C).
2. Cream butter and stir in grated cheeses.
3. In a separate bowl, mix flour, cayenne and salt. Add cheese mixture and mix well.
4. Turn mixture out on a lightly floured board and knead a few times. Divide into four portions.
5. Roll one portion out to about 1/8-inch (3 mm) — these should be rolled out thin. (Make sure there is enough flour on the board to prevent the dough from sticking.) Cut out shapes with cookie cutters and place on an ungreased cookie sheet. Repeat with remaining portions of dough.
6. Brush each shape with beaten egg, and sprinkle with nuts.
7. Bake for about 8 minutes or until golden brown. Serve warm.

Makes about 8 dozen.

YOUNG ADULT CANADIAN BOOK AWARD

These awards recognize an author of an outstanding English language Canadian book of fiction that appeals to young adults between the ages of 13 and 18.

2001
BETH GOOBIE,
Before Wings

2000
KATHERINE HOLUBITSKY,
Alone at Ninety Foot

1999
GAYLE FRIESEN,
Janey's Girl

1998
MARTHA BROOKS,
Bone Dance

1997
R.P. MACINTYRE,
Takes: Stories for Young Adults

1996
TIM WYNNE-JONES,
The Maestro

Country Meat Loaf

Don't be dismayed by the long list of ingredients — this tasty main dish is well worth the effort! The strips of pork fat used to line the pan are available at butcher shops and some supermarkets. The meat loaf can be made ahead of time and kept in the refrigerator for up to five days.

1/2 lb	chicken livers	250 g
1/3 lb	Black Forest ham	175 g
1 1/4 lb	ground lean pork	625 g
3/4 lb	ground lean veal	375 g
1/4 cup	butter	50 mL
4 cloves garlic, minced		
1/2 cup	finely chopped shallots or onions	125 mL
4 eggs, beaten		
2 juniper berries, crushed		
1 1/4 cups	coarsely chopped pecans	300 mL
2/3 cup	brandy	150 mL
1 tbsp	salt	15 mL
1 tsp	pepper	5 mL
1 tsp	dried thyme	5 mL
1 tsp	dried marjoram	5 mL
1 tsp	dried summer savory	5 mL
1 tsp	dried allspice	5 mL
pinch sage		
1/2 lb	thinly sliced fresh pork fat or bacon, cut in strips	250 g

1. Preheat oven to 350°F (180°C).
2. Trim chicken livers. Chop liver and ham into 1/2-inch (1-cm)

cubes. In large bowl, combine liver, ham, pork and veal. Set aside.

3. In a small skillet, melt butter. Cook garlic and shallots until tender, about 4 minutes. Add to meat in bowl, along with eggs, juniper berries, pecans, brandy, salt, pepper, thyme, marjoram, savory, allspice and sage. Using your hands, blend together until well mixed.

4. Line a deep 10x6-inch (3-L) loaf pan with strips of pork fat or bacon, completely covering bottom and sides of pan and leaving a slight overhang all around. Reserve a few strips to cover top. Pack meat mixture into pan, pressing to eliminate air pockets. Fold overhanging strips of pork fat over top of meat, and cover with remaining fat.

5. Cover pan tightly with foil. Place in large roasting pan and pour in enough boiling water to come halfway up sides of loaf pan. Bake for 2 1/2 hours or until loaf shrinks away from sides of pan and juices run clear.

6. Remove pan from water. Lay another pan or similar shaped container on top of the meat loaf and weigh it down with cans or jars filled with water. Leave to cool for 4 hours. Remove weight and refrigerate.

7. To serve, remove wrapping, scrape off exterior fat and cut into about 20 slices (as you would paté). Cut each slice in half.

Makes about 20 slices; serves 8 to 12.

... some children like to make castles out of the rice pudding, or faces with raisins for eyes ... Let's all play with our food, I say, and, in so doing, let us advance the state of the art together.

JULIA CHILD,
JULIA CHILD AND COMPANY, 1978

24-Hour Coleslaw

Make this tangy sweet coleslaw the day before and keep it in the refrigerator.

1 large head cabbage, cored and finely chopped		
1/2 green pepper, seeded and chopped		
1 small onion, finely chopped		
1 carrot, peeled and grated		
3/4 cup	vegetable oil	175 mL
1/2 cup	granulated sugar	125 mL
1/2 cup	cider vinegar	125 mL
1 tsp	celery seed	5 mL

1. Combine cabbage, pepper, onion and carrot in large heat-proof bowl.
2. Combine oil, sugar, vinegar and celery seed in a small saucepan or glass bowl. Bring to a full boil on top of stove or heat through in microwave. Remove from heat and pour over vegetables. Toss gently.
3. Cover and refrigerate for 24 hours before serving.

Serves 8 to 10.

Shepherd's Pie

This Mediterranean version of a traditional nursery favourite is a lamb and eggplant pot pie with a potato and feta crust.

LAMB FILLING

2 lb	eggplant	1 kg
5 tbsp	olive oil	75 mL
1 large onion, chopped		
1 tbsp	minced garlic	15 mL
2 pounds	ground lamb	1 kg
1 1/4 tsp	cinnamon	7 mL
2 tsp	crumbled dried mint	10 mL
1 1/4 tsp	crumbled dried oregano	7 mL
1/2 tsp	ground allspice	2 mL
28 oz can	Italian plum tomatoes, drained	796 mL
	(reserve 1 cup / 250 mL juice)	
2 tbsp	tomato paste	25 mL
salt and pepper to taste		
1/4 cup	freshly grated Parmesan	60 mL

POTATO TOPPING

3 lbs	baking potatoes (about 6)	1.5 kg
2 tbsp	unsalted butter	25 mL
1/3 cup	freshly grated Parmesan	75 mL
1/3 lb	crumbled feta	175 g
salt and pepper to taste		
1 tbsp	unsalted butter	15 mL

1. First make the lamb filling. Peel eggplant and cut into 1/2-inch (1-cm) slices. Place in a colander, sprinkle with salt and leave to drain for 30 minutes.

2. In a large skillet heat 4 tbsp (60 mL) of the olive oil over moderate heat. Pat the eggplant dry, and cook in batches, stirring for 15 minutes, or until it is tender but still holds its shape, and transfer it with a slotted spoon to a bowl. Set aside.

3. In the skillet heat the remaining 1 tbsp (15 mL) of olive oil over moderate heat. Cook onion, stirring, until softened. Add garlic and cook, stirring constantly, for 1 minute.

4. Add lamb and cook, stirring and breaking up any lumps, until no longer pink.

5. Pour off any excess fat. Add cinnamon, mint, oregano and allspice. Cook, stirring constantly, for 1 minute. Add tomatoes with reserved juice, tomato paste, salt and pepper and cook, stirring, for 15 minutes, or until thickened.

6. Transfer to a large bowl and stir in Parmesan. (The lamb filling will improve in flavour if made up to this point and kept, covered and chilled, overnight.)

7. To make potato topping, peel potatoes and cut into 1-inch (2.5-cm) pieces. Place in a large saucepan and cover with 1 inch (2.5 cm) water. Bring to a boil, and simmer for 10 to 15 minutes, or until potatoes are tender.

8. Drain potatoes, return to the pan and cook over moderate heat for 30 seconds, shaking the pan, to evaporate any excess liquid.

9. Force potatoes through a ricer or the medium disk of a food processor into a bowl. Add butter, Parmesan, feta, salt and pepper. Stir until mixture is well combined and butter is melted.

10. Preheat oven to 400°F (200°C). Butter a shallow 3-quart (3-L) gratin dish.

11. Add the eggplant to the lamb mixture and combine well. Spread in gratin dish. Spoon potato topping on top, spreading to cover the meat completely. Dot the surface with small pieces of butter.

12. Bake in the middle of the oven for 35 to 40 minutes, or until browned lightly.

13. If carrying as a potluck dish, reheat at 325°F (160°C) for 15 to 20 minutes.

Serves 6.

Lemon Apple Salad

This jellied salad will please both children and adults.

3 oz pkg.	lemon-flavoured gelatin	85 g
1 1/2 cups	boiling water	375 mL
1/2 cup	sour cream	125 mL
1 cup	grated apple	250 mL

1. Dissolve gelatin in boiling water by stirring well. Blend in sour cream with egg beater. Chill until partially set.
2. Fold in grated apple. Pour into ring mould if desired. Chill until set.

Makes 4 to 5 servings.

Creamy Cheese Pasta

This recipe is for adults who want a more sophisticated version of macaroni and cheese, a childhood favourite. Use any combination of cheeses you want or happen to have on hand; choose pasta that comes in smaller pieces — such as penne, fusilli, rotelli, or even macaroni.

2 cups	small pasta	500 mL
2 tbsp	butter 25 mL	
2 tbsp	all-purpose flour	25 mL
1 cup	milk 250 mL	
2 cups	crumbled cheese	500 mL
1/2 tsp	dry mustard 2 mL	
dash cumin or curry dash		
freshly ground pepper (to taste)		
1/2 cup	fresh, soft bread crumbs	125 mL
1/4 cup	freshly grated Parmesan cheese	50 mL

1. Preheat oven to 325°F (160°C). Lightly grease a baking dish.
2. Cook pasta in salted boiling water until *al dente*. Drain, and set aside.
3. Meanwhile, in a saucepan, melt butter. Add flour and stir until smooth. Pour in milk and stir until just slightly thickened.
4. Over low heat add cheese, a little at a time, stirring until well blended and smooth. If the sauce becomes too thick, add more milk. Season with mustard, cumin or curry, and pepper.
5. Place pasta in baking dish and pour cheese sauce over top. Stir carefully to coat pasta. Cover with bread crumbs and Parmesan.
6. Bake for 20 minutes or until the top is brown and sauce bubbly. If carrying as a potluck dish, reheat in oven at 325°F (160°C) for 20 minutes.

Serves 4.

Turkey Chili

Turkey adds a whole new taste to an old favourite.

1 tbsp	vegetable oil	15 mL
1 onion, peeled and chopped		
3 garlic cloves, peeled and minced		
1 red pepper, finely diced		
1 green pepper, finely diced		
1 1/2 lb	coarsely ground raw turkey breast meat	750 g
2 tbsp	all-purpose flour	25 mL
3 tbsp	chili powder	45 mL
2 tbsp	ground cumin	25 mL
2 tsp	powdered cocoa	10 mL
2 tsp	cayenne powder	10 mL
1/4 cup	tarragon vinegar	50 mL
2 tbsp	strong coffee	25 mL
28 oz can	crushed plum tomatoes	796 mL
1/4 tsp	salt	1 mL
2 cups	cooked black beans	500 mL

1. Heat oil on medium-high in a large pot or deep skillet. Add onion, garlic and peppers. Sauté, stirring frequently, for 5 minutes. Add turkey and sauté for 5 minutes, stirring constantly.

2. Stir in flour, chili powder, cumin, cocoa and cayenne. Cook over low heat, stirring frequently, for about 3 minutes.

3. Add vinegar, coffee, tomatoes and salt, and bring to a boil over medium heat. Simmer, stirring occasionally, for about 45 minutes, until chili is thick and the turkey is tender. Add beans and cook for 5 additional minutes.

4. If carrying as a potluck dish, reheat on top of stove or in microwave.

Serves 6.

Lemon Snow

This refreshing dessert is also known as Delhi Pudding.

1 1/4 cup	cold water	300 mL
3 tbsp	cornstarch	45 mL
1 tbsp	all-purpose flour	15 mL
3/4 cup	granulated sugar	175 mL
dash salt		
1/3 cup	lemon juice	75 mL
grated peel of 1/2 lemon		
2 egg whites		
1/4 cup	granulated sugar	50 mL

1. Combine water, cornstarch, flour, sugar and salt in the top of a double boiler. Cook, stirring constantly, over medium heat until thick and clear.
2. Add lemon juice and grated peel. Cook until thick and clear again. (It is impossible to overcook.)
3. Beat the egg whites until stiff. Add sugar and beat together until meringue is thick and shiny.

Note: If you have food safety concerns about uncooked eggs, combine the egg whites and sugar in a metal bowl. Set bowl over a saucepan of boiling water and beat continuously until the temperature reaches 160°F (70°C), about 5 minutes. Then proceed with the rest of the recipe.

4. Add lemon mixture to egg whites, and beat with a spoon to combine.
5. Refrigerate until serving time.

Serves 4 to 6.

Apple Upside-Down Cake

Other fruit, such as peaches, plums or pineapple, can be substituted for the apples in this versatile dessert.

3 or 4 apples		
1/2 cup	brown sugar	125 mL
1/2 cup	butter	125 mL
1/2 cup	granulated sugar	125 mL
1 egg		
1 cup	all-purpose flour	250 mL
1 1/2 tsp	baking powder	7 mL
salt (to taste)		
1/2 cup	milk	125 mL
Brown Sugar Sauce (recipe follows)		

1. Preheat oven to 350°F (180°C). Grease an 8-inch (2-L) baking dish. Dot with butter and cover bottom with brown sugar.

2. Peel and core apples, slice and arrange in baking dish.

3. Cream together butter, sugar and egg.

4. Combine flour, baking powder and salt.

5. Alternately add dry ingredients and milk to butter mixture, mixing well after each addition.

6. Pour batter on top of apples. Bake for 35 to 40 minutes.

7. To serve, pour a little Brown Sugar Sauce over each piece of cake.

Serves 10.

BROWN SUGAR SAUCE

1 tbsp	butter 15 mL
2 tbsp	all-purpose flour 25 mL
1 cup	brown sugar 250 mL
2 cups	hot water 500 mL
1 tsp	vanilla 5 mL

Combine butter, flour and sugar in a medium saucepan.
Add water and cook over low heat until thick, stirring
constantly. Cool and put in a pitcher.

Makes 1 1/2 cups (375 mL).

9 / BIOGRAPHY

GAZING INTO THE LIVES OF OTHERS

APPETIZERS

Olive Roll-Ups

Belgian Endive with Egg Salad

Salmon Ball

Ginger Sesame Eggplant Dip

MAIN COURSES

Oriental Vegetable Salad

Greek Salad

Feta and Bean Salad

Wild Mushroom & Goat Cheese Salad

with Honey Vinaigrette

DESSERTS

Mississippi Pecan Treats

Chocolate Passion Torte

Elderflower Pancakes

OPENING VISTAS

Biography is the top-selling non-fiction category (with the exception of self-help books), and there are a number of reasons for its popularity. Biography allows us a view into situations we have not personally encountered. It opens new vistas and offers a sense of connection with others. In reading biography, we examine the lives of others and look for clues that will help us comprehend our own existence. Biography reminds us of the world of the possible. It is small wonder then that some of the most memorable sessions of the book club have come when we read biography. Leaving intellectual considerations behind, another reason biography is so enjoyable is perhaps because it is, after all, a sanctified form of gossip!

The menu presented in this chapter is typical of our early summer garden parties — all main courses and salads. The elderflowers used for the historical recipe for Elderflower Pancakes are picked fresh from the garden.

THE INTREPID SURFER

Want to check up on other Canadian book clubs or register your own club? Try http://www.canadianbookclubs.com.
Can't find a recipe and the meeting is tomorrow? The folks at http://eat.epicurious.com are as "into food" as you are!

Olive Roll-Ups

These simple, delicious appetizers can be made as fiery as desired by adding more jalapeño peppers. Serve with salsa and sour cream.

8 oz	softened cream cheese	250 g
1 cup	crumbled feta cheese	250 mL
1/4 cup	chopped green olives	50 mL
1/4 cup	chopped black olives	50 mL
1/4 cup	chopped green onion	50 mL
1/2 tsp	cumin	2 mL
2–3 tbsp	diced jalapeño peppers (or to taste)	25–45 mL
4 tortilla shells		
2 tbsp	virgin olive oil	25 mL

1. Preheat oven to 350°F (175°C).
2. Combine cheeses, olives, onion, cumin and peppers. Spread mixture evenly over tortillas and roll up tightly.
3. Wrap in plastic and refrigerate at least 2 hours or up to 24 hours.
4. Cut each tortilla into 1/4-inch (1-cm) slices and arrange on a greased baking sheet. Brush with oil.
5. Bake for 12 to 15 minutes or until lightly browned. Let rest for 2 to 3 minutes before serving.

Makes about 36 pieces.

CHARLOTTE GRAY,
Sisters in the Wilderness: The Lives of Susanna Moodie and Catharine Parr Traill,
1999

The portraits of these two Canadian pioneer women positively leap from the pages of Gray's fascinating account of life in 1830s Ontario. Gray makes very real the incredible hardship they faced and the courage and perseverance they needed. She also describes the very human trials of the Moodie and Traill families with their sibling rivalry, their overambitious and depressive spouses, and their struggles with greedy and unscrupulous publishers. This biography reads like a novel and lingers in the mind long after the cover has been closed.

Belgian Endive with Egg Salad

This appetizer can be made up to four hours ahead of time and kept in the refrigerator. For an especially attractive addition to the buffet table, arrange the endive leaves in concentric circles on a large round platter. Prosciutto can be substituted for the shrimp.

4 hard-boiled eggs, finely chopped		
3 tbsp	mayonnaise	45 mL
2 tbsp	Dijon mustard	25 mL
1/2 tsp	celery salt	2 mL
6 heads Belgian endive		
4 oz	cooked bay shrimp, well drained	125 g
paprika (for garnish)		

1. Mix chopped eggs, mayonnaise, mustard and celery salt in medium bowl.
2. Cut off and discard root ends of endive. Separate leaves.
3. Place one generous teaspoon of egg mixture at wide end of each leaf, top with a shrimp and sprinkle with paprika. Arrange on a large platter, cover and chill.

Serves 12 to 14.

PETER J. CONRADI,
*Iris Murdoch:
A Life,*
2001

Iris Murdoch wrote about love, about power and about truth. She wrote about human desire and its relationship to spirituality. She also managed to cloak these lofty philosophical ideas in human form, thereby making them vivid and accessible to the ordinary reader. Conradi reveals the life of a woman perceived only as an intellectual icon, and finds her life to be "as exciting and improbable as fiction." This biography sheds light on the life of a leading thinker of the twentieth century.

Salmon Ball

Serve this tasty and attractive spread with a variety of crackers.

8 oz	cream cheese	250 g
7 1/2 oz can pink salmon		213 g
1/4 cup	chopped chives	50 mL
1/4 cup	chopped pecans	50 mL

Combine cheese, salmon and chives, and mix until fairly smooth. Form mixture into a mound on a small serving plate and cover with chopped pecans.

Serves 8.

ROSEMARY SULLIVAN,
The Red Shoes,
1998

This biography traces Margaret Atwood's personal journey from childhood to professor, editor, social activist, literary critic, poet, essayist and novelist. Sullivan parallels Atwood's intellectual development and social consciousness with North American social history between the 1940s and 1970s, arguing that Atwood is both a product of her time and an agent of change in defining the contemporary Canadian literary scene. Gracefully written and carefully researched, THE RED SHOES *reminds the reader of how Atwood has enriched Canada's literary heritage.*

Ginger Sesame Eggplant Dip

Sesame crisps or rice crackers are an excellent match for the oriental flavours of this tasty dip.

1 1/2 lb	eggplant	750 g
2 tbsp	soy sauce	25 mL
2 tbsp	brown sugar	25 mL
1 tbsp	rice vinegar	15 mL
1 tbsp	water	15 mL
1 tsp	vegetable oil	5 mL
3 cloves garlic, finely chopped		
1 tbsp	finely chopped fresh gingerroot	15 mL
4 green onions, chopped		
1/2 tsp	hot chili flakes	2 mL
1 tsp	sesame oil	5 mL
2 tbsp	chopped fresh cilantro (for garnish)	25 mL

1. Preheat oven to 425°F (250°C).
2. Pierce eggplant in several places with a fork. Roast in oven for 45 to 50 minutes or until tender. (Alternatively, microwave pierced eggplant on high for about 10 minutes.) Peel eggplant and chop finely without removing the seeds.
3. In a small bowl, combine soy sauce, sugar, vinegar and water.
4. In a wok or large skillet, heat oil on high heat. Add garlic,

ginger, green onions and chili flakes. Cook for about 30 seconds. Add soy sauce mixture. When bubbling, add eggplant. Stir to combine and heat thoroughly.

5. Remove from heat and stir in sesame oil.

6. Transfer to serving bowl and sprinkle with cilantro. Serve either cold or at room temperature.

Makes 1 1/2 cups (375 mL).

Just the knowledge that a good book is waiting for one at the end of a long day makes the day happier.

KATHLEEN NORRIS,
HANDS FULL OF LIVING,
1931

Oriental Vegetable Salad

Despite the long list of ingredients, this tasty salad is simple to prepare.

4 oz	rice noodles	125 g
enough boiling water to cover noodles		
2 tbsp	vegetable oil	25 mL
1/2 tsp	sesame oil	2 mL
1 red pepper, chopped		
4 green onions, chopped		
1 clove garlic, minced		
1 chili pepper, chopped		
2 tsp	chopped pickled ginger	10 mL
3 tbsp	soya sauce	45 mL
2 tbsp	rice wine vinegar	25 mL
1/2 cup	chopped mint	125 mL
1 tsp	chopped coriander	5 mL
1 mango, chopped		
1/2 cup	cashews	125 mL
grated zest of 1 lemon		
grated zest of 1 lime		

1. Immerse rice noodles in boiling water and leave for 2 minutes. Drain and transfer to serving bowl.
2. Add all remaining ingredients, stir to combine, and serve.

Serves 10.

Greek Salad

This traditional recipe for Greek salad is rich in Mediterranean flovours.

1 English cucumber, peeled and chopped		
3 tomatoes, chopped		
1/2 purple onion, chopped		
1/2–1 cup	crumbled feta cheese	125–250 mL
3 tbsp	olive oil	45 mL
2 tbsp	lemon juice	25 mL
salt and cracked pepper (to taste)		
1 tsp	lemon and herb seasoning	5 mL
black olives (to taste)		

Combine all ingredients in a salad bowl.
Refrigerate until ready to serve.

Serves 6.

CLARKE BLAISE,
Time Lord: The Remarkable Canadian Who Missed His Train, and Changed the World, 2001

TIME LORD describes the energetic scientific and engineering career of Sir Sandford Fleming that culminated in the establishment of a standardized worldwide system of time zones. Blaise moves beyond a straightforward biographical study of Fleming to examine the influence of new technologies on societal perceptions of time. This story of a nineteenth-century scientist who left his mark on the structure of the temporal world offers useful insights as we grapple with the new time constructs created by the computer technology.

Feta & Bean Salad

Another flavourful and easy to prepare salad.

19 oz can	red kidney beans	540 mL	
19 oz can	chickpeas	540 mL	
1 green pepper, chopped			
1 red pepper, chopped			
2–3 green onions, chopped			
1 cup	cubed feta cheese	250 mL	
1/4 cup	chopped parsley or cilantro	50 mL	
1 clove of garlic, minced			
2 tbsp	fresh lemon juice	25 mL	
1 tbsp	canola oil	15 mL	

1. Drain and rinse kidney beans and chickpeas.
2. In a salad bowl, combine beans, peas, peppers, onions, cheese, parsley and garlic.
3. Pour lemon juice and oil over top and toss.
4. Cover and refrigerate for up to 3 days.

Serves 4.

CAROLINE ALEXANDER,
**The Endurance:
Shackleton's Legendary
Antarctic Expedition,**
1998

The story of Sir Ernest Shackleton's expedition to Antarctica from 1914–16 provides sufficient danger, heroism and adventure for any armchair traveller. When Shackleton's ship, the Endurance, *is crushed by ice and sunk, he and his crew struggle for months to survive on drifting ice floes and a desolate island. A desperate voyage is made across one of the harshest oceans in the world in an attempt to reach help. No wonder this story is one of the most amazing adventures ever recorded.*

Wild Mushroom & Goat Cheese Salad with Honey Vinaigrette

This unusual salad is a SWIVEL favourite. If you prefer a little more tartness, add a squeeze of lemon just before serving.

2 heads Boston lettuce		
1 large bunch fresh spinach		
1 large head radiccio		
2 large Granny Smith apples		
8 rounds herbed goat cheese (2 oz/30 g each)		
1/2 cup	crushed walnuts or almonds	125 mL
2 cups	assorted wild mushrooms (shitake, oyster,	
	button, chanterelle and porcini, if available)	500 mL
1/4 cup	virgin olive oil	50 mL
1/4 cup	diced shallots	50 mL
3/4 cup	butter	175 mL
3 tbsp	clear honey	45 mL
2 tbsp	cider vinegar	25 mL
6 tbsp	water	90 mL
salt and freshly ground black pepper (to taste)		

1. Wash lettuce, spinach and radiccio, dry well and place in a container to transport.

NANCY MILFORD,
Savage Beauty,
2001

Edna St. Vincent Millay loved men and women, morphine and alcohol, but mostly she loved poetry. She was an avowed pacifist who ended up writing poetic propaganda to urge American participation in the Second World War. She could be wildly promiscuous, and yet she married only once, to Eugen Boissevain who remained devoted to her until his death. With meticulous research and excellent writing, Milford guides us past the frantic glamour of the 1920s and 1930s to the core of the first woman to win the Pulitzer Prize for poetry.

DENISE CHONG,
*The Concubine's Children:
Portrait of a Family
Divided,*
1994

*This is the story of Chong's
grandmother May-Ling —
a concubine brought to
Canada in the early 1900s
by the author's grandfather
— and her struggle to
survive poverty, addiction
and desertion. Chong and
her mother discover two
aunts who had been sent
back to China to be raised
by wife number one as
members of the grandfather's
first family. It is the story
of the eventual meeting of
the two halves of this
divided family.*

2. Cut apples into quarters, core. Cut each quarter into 4 or 5 wedges.

3. Coat the edges of the goat cheese rounds with crushed nuts.

4. Clean and prepare mushrooms.

5. Heat olive oil and sauté shallots and mushrooms for one minute. Add the apple wedges and sauté 1 more minute. Add butter, honey and vinegar and simmer while stirring with a wooden spoon. You should have about 1 cup of liquid — if not, add enough water to make 1 cup (250 mL) and bring to a simmer. Cool and place in small container to transport.

TO ASSEMBLE SALAD:

1. Preheat oven to 350°F (180°C).

2. Place cheese rounds on a baking sheet and bake for 4 to 5 minutes.

3. Arrange greens on a large platter, and place rounds of baked cheese on top. Using a slotted spoon, arrange mushrooms and apple wedges around the cheese rounds. Spoon dressing over salad and serve immediately.

Serves 6.

Mississippi Pecan Treats

Serve these tarts with unsweetened fresh blueberries, strawberries, raspberries, peaches or apricots.

1 cup	all-purpose flour	250 mL
1/4 cup	granulated sugar	50 mL
1/2 tsp	baking powder	2 mL
1/4 tsp	salt	1 mL
1/2 cup	cold sweet butter	125 mL
2	eggs	
1 cup	brown sugar, firmly packed	250 mL
1/4 cup	melted and cooled sweet butter	50 mL
1 tsp	vanilla	5 mL
1 cup	chopped pecans	250 mL

1. Preheat oven to 350°F (180°C).
2. To make the crust, combine flour, sugar, baking powder and salt in a bowl. With a pastry blender or two knives cut in butter until the mixture resembles coarse crumbs. Press into the bottom of an ungreased 8-inch (2-L) square pan.
3. Bake for 10 to 15 minutes, or until golden.
4. Meanwhile, make the filling. In a bowl, lightly beat eggs. Stir in sugar, butter and vanilla. Stir in pecans.
5. Spread filling over baked crust and return to oven for 20 to 25 minutes, or until puffed, golden, and almost set in centre.
6. Cool completely. Cut into 2x1-inch (5x2.5-cm) bars.

Makes 32 bars.

☙

STACY SCHIFF,
Véra
(Mrs. Vladimir
Nabokov):
A Biography,
1999

Schiff's Pulitzer Prize winning biography paints a portrait of a truly enigmatic woman: wife, muse, translator, business manager and Ideal Reader. Her account of Véra's fifty-two-year marriage to Nabokov is brilliant, witty, scholarly, readable ... and truly a love story.

☙

Chocolate Passion Torte

JAMES KING,
*The Life of Margaret
Laurence,*
1997

*This biography allows the
reader a look at the life of
one of Canada's best-known
writers. Laurence's attempts
to balance the traditional
roles of wife and mother
with her life as a writer are
both revealing and at
times touchingly sad. She
was willing to pay the
"unexpected price" required
to write, because, as
Laurence said, "What can
you do except pack up and
die?" This readable work
combines King's narrative
with excerpts of Laurence's
letters to and from
Adele Wiseman.*

How sweet it is!

CAKE

1 pkg. fudge brownie mix (21oz / 606 g)		
1/2 cup	water	125 mL
1/2 cup	oil	125 mL
2 eggs		
1 cup	coarsely chopped cream-filled chocolate sandwich cookies (about 10)	250 mL

MOUSSE

6 tbsp	water	90 mL
1 1/2 tsp	unflavoured gelatin	7 mL
1/2 cup	granulated sugar	125 mL
1/4 cup	unsweetened cocoa	50 mL
1 cup	whipping cream	250 mL
5 oz	white chocolate bar with almonds, chopped (about 1 cup/250 mL)	140 g
1/2 cup	chopped pecans, toasted	125 mL
4 cream-filled chocolate sandwich cookies, chopped		
1/2 oz	unsweetened chocolate or white chocolate (for glaze, optional)	15 g

1. Preheat oven to 350°F (180°C). Lightly grease a 10-inch (3-L) springform pan.

2. To make the cake, combine brownie mix, water, oil and eggs in a large bowl. Beat 50 strokes by hand. Stir in 1 cup (250 mL) chopped cookies. Spread in pan.

3. Bake for 40 to 50 minutes or until centre is almost set. Cool for at least 1 hour.

4. To make the mousse, place 2 tbsp (25 mL) water in a small bowl. Add gelatin and let stand 1 minute to soften. Meanwhile, in a small heavy saucepan, combine remaining 4 tbsp (60 mL) water, sugar and cocoa. Cook over medium-low heat, stirring occasionally, for 2 to 3 minutes or until sugar dissolves.

5. Reduce heat to low and add gelatin mixture. Cook, stirring constantly, until gelatin is completely dissolved. Set aside and cool to room temperature.

6. In a small bowl, beat whipping cream at medium speed until stiff peaks form. Add gelatin mixture and beat at low speed until well blended. Fold in white chocolate, pecans and 4 chopped cookies.

7. Spread mousse over the cake in springform pan.

8. If desired, melt chocolate and drizzle over the mousse in a lattice pattern.

9. Cover and chill for at least 2 hours before removing sides of pan. Store in refrigerator.

Serves 16.

TOM CONNORS,
Stompin' Tom and the Connors Tone,
2001

Stompin' Tom Connors begins the second volume of his memoirs when he is establishing his status as a Canadian legend. The book is a series of short narratives, some funny and some full of compassion, that detail his life on a weekly basis. Connors writes about spuds, hockey and places such as Sudbury and Tillsonburg — stories that resonate with many Canadians.

Elderflower Pancakes

This recipe dates back to the eighteenth century. Serve them hot with cream or yogurt.

8 elderflower heads, washed		
1 tbsp	orange-flower water	15 mL
1 tsp	ground cinnamon	5 mL
4 oz	all-purpose flour	125 mL
1/2 tsp	salt	2 mL
1/2 tsp	granulated sugar	2 mL
1 egg, separated		
1 1/4 cups milk	300 mL	
1 1/4 cups vegetable oil	300 mL	
2 tbsp	icing sugar	25 mL

1. Place elderflowers in a dish and sprinkle with orange-flower water and cinnamon.
2. Sift together flour, salt and sugar into a bowl. Add egg yolk and some of the milk. Stir well and add remaining milk. Beat batter until smooth. Whisk egg white until it forms soft peaks and fold into the batter.
3. Heat the oil in a frying pan.
4. Hold elderflowers by the stalk and dip, one at a time, into the batter, covering them completely. Place in frying pan and cook until crisp and golden, turning once.
5. Drain on paper towel and sprinkle with icing sugar.

Serves 4.

Section Four

ORGANIZING
BOOK CLUB MEETINGS
BY THEME

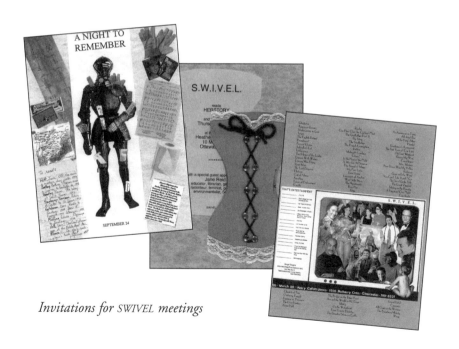

Invitations for SWIVEL meetings

10/ SANTIAGO DE COMPOSTELA
FOLLOWING IN THE FOOTSTEPS OF THE PILGRIMS

APPETIZERS

Bravas Potatoes

Toreador Meatballs

Pâté Casa Espagna

MAIN COURSES

Coquilles St-Jacques

Chicken Marbella en la Calle

Herring Salad

DESSERTS

Rainbow Ice-Cream-Sherbet Bombe

Chocolate Angel Food Cake with Chocolate Sauce

Gingered Oranges

Assorted Cheeses & Sherry*

Limonada

* Pick up at store en route to meeting

PILGRIMS FARE WITH SPANISH FLAIR

One possibility for an interesting evening is a discussion of books on a particular theme or subject. Rather than reading a single book, members focus their reading on a particular topic. At SWIVEL, we have enjoyed many evenings of animated discussion on topics as diverse as immigrants to Canada, ice and women's history. On one particularly unforgettable evening, we followed the footsteps of pilgrims through the ages on their varied journeys to Santiago de Compostela in Spain.

SAINT JAMES OF COMPOSTELA

The legend of Saint James of Compostela — the patron saint of Spain — is one of the most powerful and appealing in all of Christianity. According to tradition, after the apostle James was beheaded by Herod Agrippa in AD 44, his body was moved to the Spanish city of Santiago de Compostela, and now lies in the crypt of the cathedral. During the Middle Ages, Saint James became one of the most popular saints, but the annual pilgrimage to his shrine has been going on for more than a thousand years.

THE ROAD TO SANTIAGO — A READING LIST

Needless to say, chronicles of pilgrims along this historical route from medieval times to the present provide a rich variety of reading, as can be seen in the following list. The most popular choice was Nooteboom's *Roads to Santiago* — reminiscences of the author's several travels in Spain — but Mullins's *Pilgrimage to Santiago* — an account of the author's journey along the pilgrimage route by car — provides descriptions of architecture and pertinent historical details as well as travel information.

James Bentley, *The Way of Saint James*, 1992
Paul Coelho, *The Pilgrimage: A Contemporary Quest for Ancient Wisdom*, 1992

Laurie Dennett, *A Hug for the Apostle,* 1987

Judy Foot, *Foot by Foot to Compostella,* 1997

Nancy Frey, *Pilgrim Stories: On and Off the Road to Santiago,* 1998

Vera Hell, *The Great Pilgrimage of the Middle Ages: The Road to St. James of Compostela,* 1961

Edwin Mullins, *Pilgrimage to Santiago,* 1974

Eleanor C. Munro, *On Glory Roads: A Pilgrim's Book about Pilgrimage,* 1987

Sharan Newman, *Strong as Death,* 1996 (a pilgrimage mystery)

Cees Nooteboom, *Roads to Santiago,* 1997

Edna Poe, *Diary of a Pilgrim,* 2000

Bettina Selby, *Pilgrim's Road: A Journey to Santiago de Compostela,* 1995

THE INTREPID SURFER

The Internet is also a good source of information. For example, the Web site of the Confraternity of St. James (www.csj.org.uk) includes historical information, maps, a book list, a distance chart and answers to frequently asked questions — all the data needed to help a book club member with a busy schedule become *au courant* in the minimum of time!

It is good to have an end to journey towards; but it is the journey that matters in the end.

URSULA K. LE GUIN
THE LEFT HAND OF DARKNESS,
1969

Bravas Potatoes

This traditional Spanish tapas *can be served at room temperature.*
Tapas *are appetizers served in bars and restaurants throughout Spain to accompany sherry or cocktails. They range from a simple plate of olives or cubes of ham to quite elaborate tasty morsels.*

4 – 5 medium potatoes		
salt (to taste)		
2 cups	olive oil	500 mL
1 cup	tomato sauce	250 mL
2 tsp	mustard	10 mL
4 drops Tabasco sauce		

1. Peel potatoes and cut into medium-sized cubes. Fry for a while in warm oil, then in very hot oil to brown. Drain and sprinkle with salt.
2. Warm tomato sauce over low heat. Add mustard and Tabasco, and mix well.
3. Spread sauce over potatoes.

Serves 10.

Give me my

scallop-shell of quiet,

My staff of faith

to walk upon,

My scrip of joy,

immortal diet,

My bottle of

salvation,

My gown of glory,

hope's true gape,

And thus I'll take

my pilgrimage.

SIR WALTER RALEIGH,
THE PASSIONATE MAN'S
PILGRIMAGE,
1604

Toreador Meatballs

Take one mouthful and shout "Olé!" Take two bites and shout "Amor, eh!"
Don't forget to bring toothpicks and serviettes for these appetizers. The
ingredient quantities can be easily adjusted up or down as needed.

18 oz jar	grape jelly	500 mL
16 oz jar	chili sauce	455 mL
about 65 frozen meatballs		

1. Combine jelly and sauce and heat until blended.
2. Place unthawed meatballs in a slow cooker and pour sauce mixture on top.
3. Heat on high until ready to serve.

Serves 12.

The token carried to Santiago by pilgrims was and still is the scallop-shell ... Pilgrims also carried a staff which was useful in rough country and to ward off wild animals and savage dogs. The scrip, a soft leather wallet, carried open to receive handouts, was today's backpack. The scallop-shell was the pilgrim's dish or spoon, with which he would help himself to communal stews in hospices along the way or drink from streams, not to mention its miraculous power to cure sickness and ward off the evil eye.

ROBIN HANBURY-TENISON,
SPANISH PILGRIMAGE: A
CANTER TO ST. JAMES,
1990

Pâté Casa Espagna

The pistachios give this pâté an appealing texture.

2 tbsp	unsalted butter	25 mL
1 large onion, minced		
1 cup	brandy	250 mL
2 large garlic cloves, minced		
2 tsp	salt	10 mL
1 tsp	dried thyme	5 mL
1/2 tsp	ground pepper	2 mL
1/2 tsp	ground allspice	2 mL
3/4 pound	ground pork	475 g
3/4 pound	ground veal	475 g
2 eggs, beaten		
1/2 cup	chopped pistachios	125 mL
1 bay leaf		
8 thin bacon slices		

1. Preheat oven to 350°F (180°C).
2. Melt butter in heavy large skillet over medium heat. Add onion and sauté until golden, about 10 minutes. Transfer to a large bowl.
3. Add brandy to skillet and simmer until reduced to 1/4 cup (50 mL), about 6 minutes.
4. Pour brandy over onion. Mix in garlic, salt, thyme, pepper and allspice. Add pork, veal, eggs and pistachios, and mix well.
5. Place bay leaf in centre of 8x4-inch (1.5-L) loaf pan. Make bacon slices extra thin by holding the end of each slice

and scraping with the back of a kitchen knife. Line pan with bacon slices, arranging crosswise (allow ends to overhang the pan sides). Spoon pâté mixture into pan. Smooth the top and fold the bacon ends over top.

6. Place loaf pan in larger baking pan. Add enough hot water to come 1 1/2 inches (4 cm) up sides of loaf pan.

7. Bake about 1 1/2 hours, or until a meat thermometer inserted in the centre of the pâté registers 180°F (85°C).

8. Remove loaf pan from water and pour off any liquid from pâté. Top with foil. Place a smaller loaf pan on top of the pâté and fill with weights (cans or jars of water). Chill overnight.

9. Turn out onto platter to serve.

Serves 8.

To enter the cathedral is to sink one last time into the dream of Cluny. For though the vaults are ribbed ... the arches are Moorish and the illumination pure Romanesque, glowing and glancing off bronze, silver, intarsia, marble and painted wood; and the altar is a bonfire of dark gold. Next to it on a sort of bridge stands ... a figure of James, rougher and more like the fisherman he would have been, to which pilgrims climb to kiss its stone back.

ELEANOR MUNRO,
ON GLORY ROADS: A PILGRIM'S BOOK ABOUT PILGRIMAGE, 1987

Coquilles St-Jacques

This elegant dish combines tender, mild scallops with a fragrant wine-scented sauce. It can also be cooked and presented in individual scallop dishes. (There are about 40 scallops to the pound. Please note that frozen scallops should be thawed in the refrigerator, not at room temperature, and that thawed scallops should not be re-frozen.)

2 lb	scallops	1 kg
1 cup	water	250 mL
1 cup	dry white wine	250 mL
8 green onions, sliced		
4 celery tops		
4 sprigs of parsley		
2 bay leaves		
8 peppercorns		
1/2 tsp	thyme	2 mL
1 tsp	salt	5 mL
1 cup	sliced mushrooms	250 mL
6 tbsp	melted butter	90 mL
1/4 cup	all-purpose flour	50 mL
1 cup	18% cream	250 mL
2 egg yolks		
2 tsp	lemon juice	10 mL
1/2 cup	soft bread crumbs	125 mL
1/4 cup	grated Cheddar cheese	50 mL

1. Preheat oven to 500°F (260°C). Grease a casserole dish.
2. Wash scallops, drain and pat dry. In a pan, combine scallops,

water, wine, 4 green onions, celery, parsley, bay leaves, peppercorns, thyme and salt. Simmer for 5 minutes. Drain and reserve broth. Cut large scallops in half.

3. Sauté the other 4 green onions with mushrooms in butter. Blend in flour. Slowly add broth and stir until thickened.

4. Mix cream with egg yolks and add to sauce. Fold in scallop mixture and lemon.

5. Pour into a greased casserole dish. Bake about 15 minutes, or until bubbly.

6. Sprinkle with bread crumbs and cheese. Broil 1 to 2 minutes.

If carrying as a potluck dish, prepare recipe to step 5 but bake for about 7 minutes. Refrigerate. To serve, reheat as quickly as possible at 500°F (260°C) to bubbly stage and then complete step 6.

Serves 6 to 8.

The meal was roast pig and chips ... a specialty of the region — the pig anyway — and quite delicious, and with it we drank what was probably a local wine, though, as it came in a jug rather than a bottle, we couldn't tell ... It was so late by the time the pudding of crème caramel *... was eaten and the wine was finished that I thought I had better forego coffee in the interests of sleep, and take a little walk to shake down the rich food.*

BETTINA SELBY,
PILGRIM'S ROAD:
A JOURNEY TO SANTIAGO
DE COMPOSTELA,
1995

Chicken Marbella en la Calle

Since this piquant dish has a Spanish flair, it is perfect for a Santiago de Compostela evening. Accordingly, the dish left home under the name of "Chicken Marbella." However, as the member in question discovered, it is not a good idea to carry a hot casserole in a paper bag. The rich sauce leaked out of the dish, the paper bag gave way, and the casserole shed its mortal coil and slid onto the pavement — much to the chagrin of fellow club members and the delight of the neighbourhood dogs. And thus, this dish is now known as "Chicken Marbella en la Calle."

4 chickens, about 2 1/2 lbs each, quartered		
1 head garlic, peeled and finely pureed		
1/4 cup	dried oregano	50 mL
coarse salt and freshly ground pepper (to taste)		
1/2 cup	red wine vinegar	125 mL
1/2 cup	olive oil	125 mL
1 cup	pitted prunes	250 mL
1/2 cup	pitted Spanish green olives	125 mL
1/2 cup	capers, with a bit of the juice	125 mL
6 bay leaves		
1 cup	brown sugar	250 mL
1 cup	white wine	250 mL
1/4 cup	Italian parsley or coriander, finely chopped	50 mL

1. In a large bowl marinate chicken quarters, garlic, oregano, salt, pepper, vinegar, oil, prunes, olives, capers and bay leaves. Cover and chill in refrigerator overnight.

2. Preheat oven to 350°F (160°C).

3. Arrange chicken pieces in a single layer in one or two large, shallow pans and spoon marinade over evenly. Sprinkle with brown sugar and pour in wine.

4. Bake for 50 to 60 minutes, basting frequently with pan juices.

5. With a slotted spoon transfer chicken, prunes, olives and capers to a serving platter. Moisten with a few spoonfuls of pan juices and sprinkle generously with parsley or cilantro. Serve remaining pan juices in a sauceboat. For a potluck, this dish can be served either at room temperature or reheated in a microwave oven until bubbly.

Serves 10 to 12.

We've been to see the Apostle and we've walked 500 miles, and we won't forget the laughter, and we won't forget the smiles, and we won't forget Cirauqui, and we won't forget León; for we'd rather walk on pilgrimage than spend our life at home.

DAVID M. GITLITZ AND LINDA KAY DAVIDSON, *THE PILGRIMAGE ROAD TO SANTIAGO: THE COMPLETE CULTURAL HANDBOOK,* 2000

Herring Salad

A gentle blend of beets and potatoes flavoured with a smidgen of pickled herring in a delicate whipped cream dressing.

1 cup	whipping cream	250 mL
1 1/2 cups	cooked potatoes, diced	375 mL
1 cup	pickled beets, drained and sliced	250 mL
1 medium apple, diced		
1/2 cup	diced celery	125 mL
1/2 cup	pickled herring, drained and chopped	125 mL
1/4 cup	diced dill pickle	50 mL
1/4 cup	minced onion	50 mL
1 tsp	salt	5 mL
1/4 tsp	pepper	1 mL
2 hard-boiled eggs, cut in wedges		
parsley sprigs (for garnish)		

1. In medium bowl, whip cream until soft peaks form.
2. Gently fold in potatoes, beets, apple, celery, herring, dill pickle, onion, salt and pepper.
3. Cover with plastic wrap and refrigerate at least 6 hours.
4. To serve, arrange salad on a platter. Garnish with wedges of hard-boiled eggs and sprigs of parsley.

Serves 6.

Rainbow Ice-Cream-Sherbet Bombe

This interesting blend of ice cream and sherbet flavours is delicious either as a main dessert or as a colourful accompaniment for cakes and cookies. For best results, start the preparation the day before it is to be served. If desired, add a few drops of food colouring to tint the lemon sherbet a deeper colour.

1 1/2 pints	lemon sherbet, slightly softened	750 mL
1 1/2 pints	vanilla ice, slightly softened	750 mL
2 tbsp	green crème de menthe	25 mL
1/2 pint	raspberry sherbet, slightly softened	250 mL
1 cup	whipping cream	250 mL
2 tbsp	icing sugar	25 mL
green food colouring		

1. Lightly oil a 1 1/2-quart (1.5-L) mould, and place it in the freezer. In a large bowl, with an electric mixer, beat lemon sherbet until smooth but not melted. With a metal spatula, quickly spread sherbet evenly over the inside of the chilled mould. Freeze for 1 hour or until firm.

2. In a medium bowl, beat 1 pint vanilla ice cream with the crème de menthe. Spread ice cream evenly over lemon-sherbet layer. Freeze for 1 hour or until firm.

3. In a medium bowl, beat remaining 1/2 pint vanilla ice cream. In a small bowl, beat raspberry sherbet. Spoon raspberry sherbet into bowl with vanilla ice cream, but do not stir. Using a rubber spatula, swirl raspberry sherbet through vanilla ice cream several times. Pour into centre of mould. Freeze until firm (several hours or overnight).

Onward! Upward! "Ultrya" was the shout of encouragement — keep climbing, keep going — that pilgrims called out as they reached the Monte de Gozo (Mount of Joy) and first caught sight of the shrine of Santiago de Compostela.

4. One hour before serving, invert the mould over a serving platter. Hold a hot, damp dish cloth over mould and shake to release the bombe. Refreeze bombe until surface is firm, about 30 minutes to 1 hour.

5. In a small bowl, whip cream with icing sugar until stiff. Set aside a small amount and spoon remaining whipped cream into a pastry bag fitted with a large star tip. Decoratively pipe the cream around bottom and lengthwise across top of bombe. Pipe eight flowers onto each side of bombe. Colour the reserved whipped cream with green food colouring and pipe leaves around the flowers.

Serves 12 to 14.

Chocolate Angel Food Cake with Chocolate Sauce

This is a somewhat virtuous chocolate dessert. If you have no use for 16 to 20 egg yolks, packaged fresh egg whites are a convenient alternative.

CAKE

1 3/4 cups	granulated sugar	425 mL
1 cup	cake and pastry flour	250 mL
1/3 cup	cocoa	75 mL
2 cups	egg whites (about 16 to 20)	500 mL
1 tsp	cream of tartar	5 mL
pinch salt		
1 tsp	vanilla	5 mL

CHOCOLATE SAUCE

6 oz bitter- or semi-sweet chocolate, chopped	170 g
2 tbsp cocoa	25 mL
3 tbsp corn syrup	45 mL
1/2 cup water	125 mL
1 tsp vanilla	5 mL

1. Preheat oven to 325°F (160°C).
2. Sift 3/4 cup (175 mL) sugar three times with the flour and cocoa. Stir well. Reserve.

3. In a large bowl, beat egg whites with cream of tartar and salt until light and opaque. Slowly beat in remaining 1 cup (250 mL) sugar. Beat until stiff. Add vanilla and beat once more.

4. Fold reserved flour mixture into egg whites one third at a time. Do not overfold, but make sure there are no pockets of flour in the batter.

5. Gently turn batter into 10-inch (4-L) tube pan. Bake for 45 to 50 minutes.

6. To make chocolate sauce, combine chocolate, cocoa, corn syrup and water in saucepan and cook gently until smooth. Remove from heat and stir in vanilla. Cool. (The sauce can also be made in the microwave. Cook on high for approximately 2 minutes.)

7. Invert cake pan on rack and allow to cool for 2 hours. Remove gently from pan by running knife around edge of pan and centre tube. To serve, drizzle chocolate sauce over slices of cake.

Serves 12 to 16.

Gingered Oranges

Here is a quick, interesting and healthy dessert.

4 juice oranges (each about 8 oz/250 g)	
2 oz	fresh ginger 60 g
pinch ground cumin (optional)	

1. Peel oranges. Be careful to remove all the white pith and work over a bowl to catch any juice. Cut the oranges into 1/4-inch (.5 cm) slices and remove any seeds. Add the slices to the juice in the bowl.
2. Peel and grate the ginger and add to the oranges and juice.
3. Refrigerate until well chilled. If desired, sprinkle with cumin before serving.

Serves 4.

"Of course, modern academics will have none of the [Santiago legend]. Saint James never came to Spain ... either in his life or after his death. The story is probably a clerical fraud ... or the error of an ignorant scribe confusing the Latin for Jerusalem (Hierosolyma) *with the Latin word for Spain* (Hispania). *What's more, so the academics contend, the name Compostela has nothing to do with stars and a lot to do with a derivation of the Latin* compostum, *from which we get the phrase, compost heap."*

WILLIAM DALRYMPLE, *"WALKING TO SANTIAGO," IN TRAVELERS' TALES: SPAIN,* 1995

Limonada

This Basque lemonade is made with red and white wines.
Add more sugar if you prefer a sweeter drink.

6 lemons		
1 cup	extra fine sugar	250 mL
26 oz	dry red wine (preferably Spanish)	750 mL
26 oz	dry white wine (preferably Spanish)	750 mL

1. With a small, sharp knife or vegetable peeler, remove the yellow peel from three of the lemons. Be careful not to cut into the bitter white pith underneath. Cut the peel into strips about 2 inches long and 1/2 inch wide (5x1 cm). Set aside.

2. Squeeze juice from one of the peeled lemons. Slice the remaining 3 unpeeled lemons crosswise into 1/4-inch (.5-cm) rounds. Reserve remaining peeled lemons for another use.

3. Combine strips of peel, lemon juice, lemon slices and sugar in a 3–4-quart (3–4 L) pitcher. Add red and white wine and stir with a long-handled spoon until well mixed. Refrigerate for at least 8 hours, stirring two or three times.

4. Stir again, taste for sweetness, and pour into chilled wine glasses or tumblers. If you like, fill glasses with ice cubes before adding the limonada.

Serves 8.

11/ SWIVEL GOES TO THE MOVIES

READ THE BOOK ... REVIEW THE FILM

APPETIZERS

California Melt
Crème Fraîche (Fruit Dip)

MAIN COURSES

Saumon Fumé
Salad Niçoise
Hawaiian Chicken
Waldorf Salad
Cactus Salad

DESSERTS

Pavlova
White Pepper & Lemon Ginger Rogers Cake
Elvis Presley Cake
Hello Dolly Squares
Almond Squares
Crunchy Chocolate Bar Dessert

STUDYING THE STARS

An evening devoted to discussing a film based on a novel or a short story is an obvious digression for a book club. Indeed, for busy club members, it will serve as a respite from the regular reading regime — and (as long as you have read the novel) an opportunity to prepare for the next meeting in a single evening. Discussion of the merits and drawbacks of the novel versus the film can be engaging and active as readers balance the supremacy of the written word against the visuals of film. At the end of the evening, it is likely that everyone will admit that both mediums have their virtues.

The sidebars in this chapter present a number of films based on well-known novels. Most of these films should be readily available at your local video rental.

California Melt

Now that's surfin'!

1 French-style baguette		
1/2 cup	Sun-Dried Tomato Paste (recipe follows)	125 mL
1 cup	Guacamole (recipe follows)	250 mL
4 oz	ripened brie, cut in thin slices	125 g

1. Split baguette in half lengthwise.
2. Spread sun-dried tomato paste and then guacamole over cut side of each half. Cover with slices of brie.
3. Broil for 3 to 5 minutes or until brown and bubbly.

Serves 6 to 8.

SUN-DRIED TOMATO PASTE

2 oz	sun-dried tomatoes (not oil-packed)	60 g
2 tbsp	olive oil	25 mL
1/3 cup	Parmesan cheese	75 mL
1 clove garlic, minced		

Soak tomatoes in boiling water for 2 minutes. Drain and cut into small pieces. Combine with oil, cheese and garlic to make a paste.

Makes 1/2 cup (125 mL).

THE COLOR PURPLE, *1985*

A film by Steven Spielberg
Based on the novel by
Alice Walker (1982)

Screenplay
by Menno Mayjes

Starring
Oprah Winfrey,
Danny Glover,
Whoopi Goldberg,
Adolph Caesar,
Akosua Busia

HOWARD'S END,
1992

*A film by James Ivory
and Rob Cohen
Based on the novel by
E.M.Forster (1910)*

*Screenplay by
Ruth Prawer Jhabvala*

*Starring
Emma Thompson,
Helena Bonham Carter,
Vanessa Redgrave,
Anthony Hopkins*

GUACAMOLE

2 ripe avocados		
1 clove garlic, minced		
2 tbsp	lime juice	25 mL
1/4 cup	finely chopped onion	50 mL
2 tbsp	minced jalapeño chilies	25 mL
salt and pepper (to taste)		

Mash avocado, garlic and lime juice together. Add onion, chilies, salt and pepper and mix well.

Makes 1 cup.

Crème Fraîche (Fruit Dip)

Help me, Rhonda! Crème fraîche makes a divine dip for fresh fruit and it can also be used for thickening sauces and soups. Food basted with it broils beautifully! Crème fraîche will keep for up to two weeks in the refrigerator. It is available at most dairy counters, but to make it yourself ...

2 cups	whipping cream	500 mL
1 cup	yogurt	250 mL

1. Combine cream and yogurt in a medium-sized saucepan. Stir well, and heat to 175°F (80°C). Make sure the temperature is no higher.
2. Pour yogurt mixture into a container, partially cover, and leave at room temperature for 6 to 8 hours, or until the mixture has thickened and tastes slightly acidic.
3. Cover and refrigerate.

Makes 1 cup (250 mL).

THE COMMITMENTS,
1991

*Based on the novel by
Roddy Doyle (1988)*

*Directed by
Alan Parker*

*Screenplay by
Dick Clement, Roddy Doyle,
Ian Le Fremais*

*Starring
Andrew Strong, Bronagh
Gallagher, Angeline Ball,
Colm Meaney,
Dave Finnegan*

Saumon Fumé

Serve this French connection with crackers or thin slices of baguette.

THE DIVINERS,
1993

Based on the novel by
Margaret Laurence (1974)

Directed by
Anne Wheeler

Screenplay by
Margaret Laurence

Starring
Sonja Smits,
Wayne Robson,
Diane Douglas,
Tom Jackson,
Don Francks,
Doreen Brownstone

2 or 3 sprigs fresh dill		
1/4 cup	butter	50 mL
8 oz	cream cheese	250 g
2 tbsp	chopped fresh dill	25 mL
1/4 lb	sliced smoked salmon	125 g

1. Line a plain mould with plastic wrap. Arrange dill sprigs on the bottom.
2. Beat butter and cream cheese together. Spread a third of this mixture in the mould. Sprinkle with half of chopped dill and top with half of the salmon.
3. Repeat layers, ending with cream cheese mixture. Press down lightly to compact layers.
4. Cover with plastic wrap and chill overnight.
5. To serve, remove plastic wrap, dip mould in hot water for a few seconds. Invert onto a plate, and garnish as desired.

Serves 6.

Salad Niçoise

This popular combination of Mediterranean produce and flavours is a staple at Cannes. Arrange the salad on a large platter and let everyone help themselves. Pass the vinaigrette separately.

3 medium potatoes, unpeeled		
3 eggs		
16 oz can	French-style green beans, drained	500 g
	(or 1/4 lb/120 g fresh green beans)	
2 medium tomatoes, cut into wedges		
12 oz	canned tuna (or grilled tuna steak)	375 g
2 oz	anchovy fillets	5 g
2 small heads Boston lettuce		
6 oz	pitted ripe olives	170 g
Vinaigrette (recipe follows)		

1. Cook potatoes until fork-tender. Hard boil the eggs. Steam fresh beans (if using) until tender but still crisp. Refrigerate cooked potatoes, eggs and beans until thoroughly chilled.

2. Begin to assemble salad about 45 minutes before serving. Peel potatoes and cut into bite-sized pieces. Peel hard-boiled eggs and cut into 4 wedges. Cut tomatoes into wedges.

3. Drain tuna (if canned) and separate into bite-sized pieces. Drain anchovies and separate the fillets.

4. Tear lettuce into bite-sized pieces and place in large salad bowl or on a platter. Arrange potatoes, tuna, eggs, tomatoes, beans and anchovies in separate piles on top of lettuce. Garnish with olives and vinaigrette.

Serves 4.

THE ENGLISH
PATIENT,
1996

*A film by Anthony Minghella
Based on the novel by
Michael Ondaatje (1992)*

*Screenplay by
Anthony Minghella and
Michael Ondaatje*

*Starring
Ralph Fiennes,
Juliette Binoche,
Kristin Scott Thomas,
Willem Dafoe,
Colin Firth*

ANGELS AND
INSECTS,
1996

*A film by Philip Hass
Adapted by Philip and
Belinda Haas from
the A.S. Byatt novella*
MORPHO EUGENIA
(1992)

*Starring
Mark Rylance,
KristinScott Thomas,
Patsy Kensit,
Jeremy Kemp,
Anna Massey*

VINAIGRETTE

2/3 cup	olive oil 150 mL
1/4 cup	red wine vinegar 50 mL
1 tsp	salt 5 mL
1/2 tsp	chervil 2 mL
1/2 tsp	tarragon 2 mL
1/8 tsp	pepper .5 mL

Combine all ingredients in a small bowl and whisk until well blended.

Makes 1 cup.

Hawaiian Chicken

This recipe works well with long-cooking rice, but not instant.

4 chicken breasts, boned and skinned		
1 medium-sized Spanish onion, finely chopped		
2 tbsp	vegetable oil	25 mL
2 1/2 cups	chicken broth	625 mL
14 oz can	pineapple tidbits in juice, undrained	430 g
1 1/2 cups	uncooked long-grain white rice	375 mL
3/4 cup	finely chopped carrots	175 mL
1/2 cup	chopped green pepper	125 mL
1/2 cup	chopped sweet red pepper	125 mL
1/3 cup	ketchup	75 mL
2 tbsp	brown sugar	25 mL
2 tbsp	soy sauce	25 mL
2 tbsp	white vinegar	25 mL
2 cloves garlic, minced		
3/4 cup	chopped green onions	175 mL

1. Cut chicken into 1-inch (2.5-cm) cubes.

2. In a large skillet or Dutch oven, sauté onion in oil until soft. Add chicken and cook over medium-high heat until the meat is no longer pink.

3. Add broth, pineapple, rice, carrots, peppers, ketchup, brown sugar, soy sauce, vinegar and garlic. Stir well to combine.

4. Bring to a boil, reduce heat to medium-low, cover and simmer for 25 minutes or until rice is tender. Stir occasionally. Stir in green onions during the last five minutes of cooking time.

Serves 4.

❧

REGENERATION,
1998

*Based on the novel by
Pat Barker (1991)*

*Screenplay by
Alan Scott*

*Directed by Gillies
MacKinnon*

*Starring
Jonathan Pryce,
James Wilby,
Jonny Lee Miller,
David Hayman,
Stuart Bunce*

❧

Waldorf Salad

"Peel me a grape, Hortense."

1 cup	mayonnaise	250 mL
1/4 cup	lemon juice	50 mL
1 lb	red eating apples	500 g
2 cups	thinly sliced celery	500 mL
1 cup	chopped walnuts	250 mL
1 cup	dark seedless raisins	250 mL
lettuce leaves (for salad base)		

1. In medium bowl, mix mayonnaise and lemon juice.
2. Core and dice apples. Add to mayonnaise mixture and stir to coat well.
3. Add celery, walnuts and raisins. Toss gently to combine.
4. To serve, arrange lettuce leaves on serving platter and spoon salad into the centre.

Serves 8.

Cactus Salad

The good, the pad and the vinaigrette! Nopales are the fleshy, oval-shaped leaves of the nopal (or prickly pear) cactus. Fresh nopales are sometimes available, but the canned variety — cut in pieces or strips and either pickled or packed in water — known as nopalitos will likely be easier to find.

16 oz can or jar nopalitos, drained and rinsed		454 g
4 medium tomatoes		
1–2 tbsp	fresh cilantro leaves	15–25 mL
1/2 medium Spanish onion		
1/3 cup	olive oil (or to taste)	75 mL
3 tbsp	vinegar (or to taste)	45 mL
salt (to taste)		

1. Drain and rinse nopalitos. Place in bowl.
2. Chop tomatoes, cilantro and onion, and add to nopalitos.
3. Dress with olive oil, vinegar and salt. Toss and enjoy.

Serves 6.

THE CIDER HOUSE
RULES,
1999

*Adapted by John Irving
from his novel (1985)*

*Directed by
Lasse Hallström*

*Starring
Tobey Maguire,
Charlize Theron,
Michael Caine,
Delroy Lindo,
Paul Rudd*

Pavlova

Put this treat into your tucker bag for the next club meeting. Use kiwi fruit, strawberries, raspberries or blueberries, or a combination of any two or more. If whipped cream is too rich to consider, substitute the extra-thick, Greek-style yogurt for half the cream. Add 1 tsp (5 mL) gelatin to the yogurt before folding it into the whipped cream.

~

THE DIVINE
RYANS,
1999

A film by Stephen Reynolds
Based on the novel by
Wayne Johnson (1990)

Starring
Marguerite MacNeil,
Mary Walsh,
Peter Postlethwaite,
Rick Boland,
Robert Joy

~

4 egg whites		
1 cup	granulated sugar	250 mL
2 tsp	white vinegar	10 mL
1 tbsp	corn starch	15 mL
1 1/2 cups	whipping cream	375 mL
3 cups	fruit	750 mL

1. Preheat oven to 275°F (140°C). Line a cookie sheet with parchment or foil.
2. In a clean glass bowl, beat egg whites with an electric mixer until soft peaks form. Add sugar gradually, beating well after each addition. Add vinegar and corn starch and beat until the mixture is very stiff and shiny.
3. Mound meringue mixture on prepared cookie sheet and form into a disc shape about 8 inches (20 cm) in diameter and 2 inches (5 cm) high.
4. Bake for 1 1/2 to 2 hours or until the meringue is crisp and dry and creamy in colour. Let cool and then slide onto a serving platter.
5. Whip cream until stiff peaks form. Just before serving, spread over meringue and decorate with fruit. (If you add the cream and fruit too early, the meringue will soften.)

Serves 8.

White Pepper & Lemon Ginger Rogers Cake

Serve with a dash of Fred Astaire!

1/4 cup	fine, dry breadcrumbs	50 mL
2 tbsp	lemon juice	25 mL
zest of 2 large lemons, finely grated		
1/2 x 1-inch piece of ginger	1.25 x 2.5-cm	
1 cup	unsalted butter	250 mL
1 3/4 cups granulated sugar	425 mL	
3 large eggs		
3 cups	sifted all-purpose flour	750 mL
1 tbsp	baking soda	15 mL
3/4 tsp	baking powder	4 mL
1/2 tsp	salt	2 mL
1 tsp	white pepper	5 mL
1 cup	buttermilk	250 mL
1/2 cup	lemon juice (for glaze)	125 mL
1/2 cup	granulated sugar (for glaze)	125 mL

1. Set rack at bottom third of the oven. Preheat oven to 325°F (160°C). Butter a tube pan, dust with breadcrumbs, and shake out excess crumbs.

2. In a small cup, combine lemon juice and zest. Grate the ginger and add.

3. In a large bowl, beat butter until soft. Add sugar and beat about 1 minute. Add eggs, one at a time, beating well after each addition.

☙

A MAP OF THE WORLD, *1999*

*A film by Scott Elliot
Based on the novel by
Jane Hamilton (1994)
Adapted by Peter Hedges
and Polly Platt*

*Starring
Sigourney Weaver,
Julianna Moore,
David Starthaim*

☙

Ginger Rogers did everything that Fred Astaire did. She just did it backwards and in high heels.

VARIOUSLY ATTIRBUTED TO
FAITH WHITTLESEY,
LINDA ELLERBEE
AND ANN RICHARDS,
1980s.

4. Sift together flour, baking soda, baking powder, salt and pepper.

5. While beating on low speed, add dry ingredients to the butter mixture in thirds, alternating with buttermilk. Add ginger-lemon mixture and stir to combine.

6. Pour batter into pan and smooth the top. Bake for 1 1/4 hours.

7. Immediately after putting the cake in the oven, combine lemon juice and sugar for the glaze. Stir until sugar is dissolved. Let stand.

8. The cake is done when a skewer inserted into the centre comes out clean. Remove from oven. Let rest on a wire rack for 5 minutes, then invert onto rack.

9. Place rack over a sheet of foil. Brush all top surfaces of the cake (including tube hole) with the lemon glaze. (Brush up any drips of glaze from the foil and apply it to cake.) The cake will absorb all glaze. When cool, transfer cake to a plate.

Serves 14.

Elvis Presley Cake

Shake, rattle and bake!

1 cup	mayonnaise	250 mL
1 cup	granulated sugar	250 mL
2 cups	all-purpose flour	500 mL
1/2 tsp	salt	2 mL
2 tsp	baking soda	10 mL
4 tbsp	cocoa	60 mL
1 cup	hot water	250 mL
1 tsp	vanilla	5 mL

1. Preheat oven to 350°F (180°C). Grease an 8-inch (2-L) square cake pan.

2. Combine mayonnaise and sugar and beat until smooth.

3. Sift together flour, salt and baking soda. Stir into mayonnaise mixture.

4. Dissolve cocoa in hot water and add vanilla. Stir into batter.

5. Pour batter into pan. Bake for 40 to 50 minutes, or until a skewer inserted into the centre comes out clean.

Serves 6 to 8.

CHOCOLAT,
2000

*A film by Lasse Hallström
and screenwriter
Robert Nelson Jacob
Based on the novel by
Joan Harris
(2000)*

*Starring
Juliette Binoche,
Lena Olin,
Judi Dench,
Alfred Molina,
Johnny Depp*

Hello Dolly Squares

A dessert guaranteed to satisfy your sweet tooth!

1/4 cup	butter	50 mL
1 cup	graham wafer crumbs	250 mL
1 cup	coconut	250 mL
1 cup	chocolate chips	250 mL
1 cup	chopped pecans or walnuts	250 mL
1 1/4 cups	sweetened condensed milk	300 mL

1. Preheat oven to 350°F (180°C).
2. Melt butter in an 8x8-inch (2-L) cake pan. Add crumbs, mix to combine, and press into bottom of pan.
3. Add coconut, chocolate chips, nuts and condensed milk in layers.
4. Bake for 30 minutes.
5. Cool pan on rack, and cut into squares.

Makes 24 squares.

Almond Squares

Delectably delicious!

30 graham wafers		
1 cup	brown sugar	250 mL
1 1/2 cups butter		375 mL
2 cups	sliced almonds	500 mL

1. Preheat oven to 400°F (200°C).
2. Line a 12x19-inch (31x48-cm) cookie sheet with whole graham wafers.
3. In a small saucepan, melt brown sugar and butter. When the mixture starts to boil, pour over the wafers. Cover with almonds.
4. Bake for 8 minutes. Watch carefully to make sure it does not burn.
5. Cut into squares while still hot. Cool and refrigerate.

Makes 36 squares.

∞

LOST AND
DELIRIOUS,
2001

A film by Lea Pool
Based on the novel
The Wives of Bath
by Susan Swan (1993)

Screenplay by
Judith Thompson

Starring
Piper Perabo,
Misha Barton, Jessica Pare,
Jackie Burroughs,
Caroline Dhavernas,
Graham Greene

∞

Crunchy Chocolate Bar Dessert

2 good 2 B 4-gotten! Mix and match the chocolate bars and pudding mixes.

1 large angel food cake		
1 pkg instant butterscotch pudding (4 oz/136 g)		
1 2/3 cup	water	400 mL
1/2 tsp	instant coffee	2 mL
1 tsp	maple syrup	5 mL
2 crunchy chocolate bars (2 oz/60 g each)		
2 cups	whipped-cream topping	500 mL

1. Cut cake horizontally into 4 layers.
2. Mix contents of package with water, coffee and maple syrup, stirring constantly over medium heat until mixture boils. Let cool.
3. Crush 1 chocolate bar.
4. Place half of the topping in a bowl and fold in pudding and crushed chocolate bar.
5. Place one cake layer in a serving dish and cover with one quarter of the pudding mixture. Repeat with remaining cake layers, ending with cake on the top. Cover with plastic wrap and chill for several hours. Reserve remaining mixture.
6. Remove plastic wrap, spread remaining topping over the cake. Crush second chocolate bar and use to decorate the top.

Serves 6 to 8.

I'll be eighty this month. Age, if nothing else, entitles me to set the record straight before I dissolve. I've given my memoirs far more thought than any of my marriages. You can't divorce a book.

GLORIA SWANSON
THE NEW YORK TIMES,
1979

222

12/ HERSTORY

SEEING THE PAST
THROUGH WOMEN'S EYES

DESSERTS

Bavarian Apple Torte

Caramel Pecan Brownies

Mocha Mousse

Rhubarb-Strawberry Streusel

Coffee Cake

Glazed Choclate Delight

Saucy Fudge Pudding

Raspberry Pie

Julie's Lemon Dessert

ABCD Maple Mousse

Key Lime Pie

Rewriting the Record

"If we are women, we look back through our mothers."

Virginia Woolf,
A Room of One's Own, 1928

Until the expansion of the women's movement in the 1970s, historians had been overwhelmingly male, and history was almost exclusively a recounting of great deeds done by great men. Most women's lives were considered trivial and unimportant by the predominantly male gaze of history. Women's history undertook to re-vision history in order to specifically seek out and record women's lives and activities. The reinsertion of women into the historical record has allowed women to see evidence of their existence as historical agents and participants. It has allowed women to use the knowledge and wisdom of their foremothers to interpret the present and envision the future. Knowing that the great majority of book club members are female, we created this chapter on "herstory." In the sidebars, we suggest a selection of Canadian, American and British works that present a particularly female vision of significant events that allow all of us, both women and men, "to look back through our mothers."

THE INTREPID SURFER

There are two Internet sites where you can find a great selection of biographies and related readings about Canadian women: the "More Features" section of Coolwomen at www.coolwomen.ca, and the "Celebrating Women's Achievements" page at the National Library of Canada, www.nlc-bnc.ca. For links to women's history resources from around the world, visit Virtual Library Women's History at www.iisg.nl.

Bavarian Apple Torte

This is a simple but delicious torte.

1/2 cup	margarine	125 mL
1/3 cup	granulated sugar	75 mL
1/4 tsp	vanilla	1 mL
1 cup	all-purpose flour	250 mL
8 oz	cream cheese	250 g
1/4 cup	granulated sugar	50 mL
1 egg		
1/2 tsp	vanilla	2 mL
1/3 cup	granulated sugar	75 mL
1/4 tsp	cinnamon	1 mL
4 cups	sliced apples	1 L
1/4 cup	slivered almonds	50 mL

1. Preheat oven to 450°F (225°C). Grease a 9-inch (2.5-L) springform pan.

2. Cream together margarine, 1/3 cup (75 mL) sugar and vanilla. Blend in flour. Spread on bottom and sides of pan.

3. Combine cream cheese, 1/4 cup (50 mL) sugar, egg and vanilla. Spread over pastry.

4. Combine 1/3 cup (75 mL) sugar and cinnamon. Add apples and toss to coat, then spoon over cheese layer. Sprinkle with slivered almonds.

5. Bake at 450°F (240°C) for 10 minutes. Reduce heat to 400°F (200°C) and bake for 25 minutes.

6. Cool on rack. Serve at room temperature.

Serves 6 to 8.

SHARON ANNE COOK, LORNA R. MCLEAN AND KATE O'ROURKE, EDS.,

Framing Our Past: Canadian Women's History in the Twentieth Century, 2001

The 85 short essays and 225 photographs in this coffee-table book document women's vast contribution to Canada's past. Facets of Canadian women's history are examined through everyday events — social rituals, athletic activities, philanthropic, spiritual and aesthetic pursuits (such as landscape painting and study and reading groups), nurturing, teaching and working in professional, minimally-paid and unpaid settings.

Caramel Pecan Brownies

This decadent combination of chocolate and caramel will enchant chocolate lovers. These brownies can be wrapped in foil and stored at room temperature for up to five days or frozen in an airtight container for up to one month.

2 oz	milk chocolate bar with caramel centre	60g
4 oz	bitter- or semi-sweet chocolate, chopped	125 g
2 oz	unsweetened chocolate, chopped	60 g
1/2 cup	cold butter, cut in cubes	125 mL
1 cup	granulated sugar	250 mL
1 tsp	vanilla	5 mL
2 eggs		
3/4 cup	all-purpose flour	175 mL
1/4 tsp	baking powder	1 mL
pinch salt		
1/2 cup	chopped toasted pecans	125 mL
2 tbsp	butterscotch sauce (optional)	25 mL

1. Preheat oven to 350°F (180°C). Line an 8-inch (2-L) square cake pan with foil, leaving an overhang for handles on opposite sides of the pan; grease the foil. Set aside.

2. Cut caramel chocolate bar squares into quarters and set aside.

3. In a heavy saucepan over low heat, melt bittersweet and unsweetened chocolate with the butter, stirring constantly. Remove from heat and cool slightly. (Alternatively, microwave chocolate and butter on medium for about three minutes.

Do not cover. Microwave times will vary. Watch carefully and stir frequently. Stop cooking as soon as all chocolate pieces are melted.)

4. Whisk sugar and vanilla into the melted chocolate. Whisk in eggs, one at a time, beating until the mixture is shiny.

5. In a bowl, combine flour, baking powder and salt with half of the pecans. Stir gently into chocolate mixture until just combined. Scrape batter into prepared pan.

6. Drizzle with half the butterscotch sauce. Scatter remaining pecans and caramel chocolate pieces over top; lightly press into batter without submerging. Drizzle with remaining sauce.

7. Bake in centre of oven for 35 minutes or until tester inserted in centre comes out clean.

8. Cool in pan on rack. Using foil handles, lift brownies out of pan and cut into squares.

Makes 30 squares.

Mocha Mousse

Have several copies of the recipe on hand whenever you serve this amazingly simple, elegant, delicious dessert, because it's sure to be a hit! It is best made a day ahead.

4 tsp	instant coffee	20 mL
1 cup	boiling water	250 mL
16 oz	regular marshmallows	454g
8 oz pkg.	chocolate wafers	250 g
1/4 cup	melted butter	50 mL
1 cup	whipping cream	250 mL

1. Dissolve instant coffee in boiling water. Add marshmallows and stir over low heat until smooth. Refrigerate for 1 hour.

2. Arrange 14 wafers around the edge of a 10-inch (4-L) springform pan. Crush remaining wafers, combine with the melted butter, and pat into pan. Chill.

3. Whip the marshmallow mixture to make sure it is well blended. Whip 3/4 cup (175 mL) of the cream and fold into marshmallow mixture. Pour over wafer mixture in pan and chill until serving time.

4. Just before serving, remove from pan, whip remaining 1/4 cup (50 mL) cream, sweeten to taste and spread on top. Garnish with a few wafer crumbs.

Serves 8.

Rhubarb-Strawberry Streusel Coffee Cake

A simple but delicious coffee cake. If you are short of either time or fresh fruit, substitute one 19-oz (540-mL) can of cherry, apple or blueberry pie filling and (if desired) 1/3 cup (75 mL) raisins for the homemade filling. To sour milk, add 1 tbsp (15 mL) vinegar or lemon juice to 3/4 cup (175 mL) milk and let sit for 10 minutes.

FILLING

3/4 cup	granulated sugar	175 mL
2 tbsp	all-purpose flour	25 mL
1 tsp	cinnamon	5 mL
3 cups	coarsely chopped rhubarb	750 mL
2 cups	sliced strawberries	500 mL

CAKE

2 1/4 cups	all-purpose flour	550 mL
3/4 cup	granulated sugar	175 mL
3/4 cup	butter	175 mL
1/2 tsp	baking powder	2 mL
1/2 tsp	baking soda	2 mL
1 egg, beaten		
3/4 cup	sour milk	175 mL

1. Preheat oven to 400°F (200°C). Grease a 9-inch (2.5-L) spring-form pan.
2. To make the filling, combine sugar, flour and cinnamon in a bowl.

JILL KER CONWAY,
True North,
1994

Conway, an Australian who became the first female vice-president of the University of Toronto, and later the first female president of Smith College, recounts her education at Radcliffe College and her subsequent work and life in Toronto. This book is an interesting and moving description of Conway's rejection of the subordinate status ascribed to women of her generation coupled with her search for personal fulfillment.

Add rhubarb and strawberries and toss to mix.

3. Spread mixture in an 8-cup (2-L) shallow glass baking dish. Bake for 10 minutes. The fruit should have the consistency of pie filling and should measure about 2 cups (500 mL). Remove from oven and reduce oven temperature to 350°F (180°C).

4. To make the cake, combine flour and sugar in large bowl. Cut in butter until the mixture resembles fine crumbs. Set aside 1/2 cup (125 mL) of this mixture. To the remainder, add baking powder and baking soda.

5. Combine egg and sour milk. Add to dry ingredients and stir until just moistened. Spread two-thirds of this batter over the bottom and part way up sides of springform pan. Spoon fruit filling over batter. Top with spoonfuls of remaining batter and sprinkle with reserved crumb mixture.

6. Bake for 50 to 55 minutes.

Serves 12.

Glazed Chocolate Delight

If chocolate is your passion, this is your recipe. Just before serving, decorate the cake with edible flowers or another garnish of your choice.

CAKE

1/4 cup	butter	50 mL
4 oz	semi-sweet chocolate	125 g
4 eggs, separated		
1/2 cup	granulated sugar	125 mL
1/3 cup	cocoa	75 mL
1/4 cup	orange liqueur	50 mL

GLAZE

4 oz	semi-sweet chocolate	125 mL
2 tbsp	orange liqueur	25 mL
1/4 cup	butter	50 mL

1. Preheat oven to 325°F (160°C). Lightly butter an 8-inch (2-L) springform pan and line the bottom with parchment paper.

2. To make the cake, melt butter and 4 oz (125 g) of chocolate together. Let cool. (Alternatively, microwave chocolate and butter at medium for approximately three minutes. Do not cover. Microwave times will vary. Watch carefully and stir frequently. Stop cooking as soon as the chocolate pieces have melted.)

3. Beat egg yolks with 1/4 cup (50 mL) sugar. Add chocolate mixture, cocoa powder and orange liqueur and mix well.

4. Beat egg whites until soft peaks form. Add remaining 1/4 cup (50 mL) sugar and beat until stiff peaks form. Fold meringue

VERONICA STRONG-BOAG,
The New Day Recalled: Lives of Girls and Women in English Canada, 1919–1939,
1988

Strong-Boag's history of Canadian women in the interwar period is one of the most readable examples of recent and original women's history. By tracing the life courses of women through childhood, courtship and marriage, domestic and paid work, motherhood and aging, she examines what it meant to be a woman during a period when most of our grandmothers and mothers were forming their values.

NUALA O'FAOLAIN,
Are You Somebody:
The Accidental Memoir of
a Dublin Woman,
1998

This memoir, by a columnist
for The Irish Times, captures
the author's search for truth,
love and knowledge. It also
casts a critical eye on the
society which surrounds
her. Roddy Doyle has
commented that in "writing
about herself, Nuala
O'Faolain has also written
about Ireland. It is a
cruel, wounded place —
and this book has became
an important part of
the cure."

into chocolate mixture and pour into pan.

5. Bake at 325°F (160°C) for 30 to 35 minutes. Cool on rack.

6. While cake is baking, prepare glaze. Combine chocolate, orange liqueur, and butter in a double boiler and heat until melted and blended. Cool to room temperature.

7. Invert cake on a serving plate. Spread with glaze and refrigerate until the glaze is firm.

Serves 8 to 10.

Saucy Fudge Pudding

This "one-bowl pleasure" has a charming chocolate sauce bottom.

1 cup	all-purpose flour	250 mL
3/4 cup	granulated sugar	175 mL
2 tbsp	cocoa	25 mL
2 tsp	baking powder	10 mL
1/4 tsp	salt	1 mL
1/2 cup	milk	125 mL
2 tbsp	cooking oil or melted butter	25 mL
1/2 cup	chopped nuts (optional)	125 mL
3/4 cup	brown sugar, packed	175 mL
2 tbsp	cocoa	25 mL
1 3/4 cups	hot water	425 mL

1. Preheat oven to 350° F (180° C).

2. Combine flour, sugar, cocoa, baking powder and salt in a medium bowl. Stir to mix.

3. Add milk, oil and nuts. Mix together well and press into an 8-inch (2-L) casserole or pan.

4. In original bowl, combine brown sugar and cocoa. Add hot water and stir until sugar is dissolved.

5. Pour over batter in pan, but do not stir. Bake uncovered for about 40 minutes or until the batter has risen above sauce and is firm to the touch.

Serves 6.

Maria Tippett,
*Emily Carr:
A Biography,*
1979

Tippett's ground-breaking work on this well-known Canadian artist is clearly and dramatically written, using a wide variety of historical sources and incisive analysis. Drawing on both the substantial body of written work produced by Carr and her paintings, Tippett recreates the life of Emily Carr as she lived it, not as she told it to others.

Raspberry Pie

Fruit pies are traditional Canadian fare. Make this one when raspberries are fresh and plentiful (and not too expensive). You can either bake it right away or freeze it for baking at a later date. Alternatives to the traditional scoop of ice cream on the side include a dollop of yogurt (for the sanctimonious), a dab of whipped cream (for those who are not calorie-conscious), or for added zip, a thin slice of sharp Canadian Cheddar.

6 cups	cake and pastry flour	1.5 L
	(or 5 1/2 cups/ 1.4 L all-purpose flour)	
1 tsp	salt	5 mL
1 tbsp	baking powder	15 mL
1 lb	lard	500 g
1 tbsp	vinegar	15 mL
1 egg, lightly beaten		
cold water		
4 cups	fresh ripe raspberries	1 L
1 cup	granulated sugar	250 mL
2 tbsp	minute tapioca	25 mL
1 tbsp	sugar mixed with 1 tbsp (15 mL) milk	15 mL
	(to use with frozen pie)	

1. Preheat oven to 425°F (220°C).
2. Mix together flour, salt and baking powder. Cut in lard with pastry blender or 2 knives until mixture resembles coarse oatmeal.
3. In a 1-cup (250-mL) measure, combine vinegar and egg. Add enough water to make 1 cup (250 mL). Gradually stir liquid into flour mixture, adding only enough liquid to make

the dough cling together.

4. Form dough into a ball and divide into 6 portions. Wrap 4 portions and refrigerate or freeze for later use.

5. Roll out one portion on a lightly floured surface. (If dough is sticking, chill 1 to 2 hours.) Transfer dough to 9-inch (23-cm) glass pie plate and trim the edges. Roll out second portion for top crust.

6. Gently mix raspberries, sugar and tapioca, and place in pie shell. Cover with top crust and trim edges. Gently press the tines of a fork dipped in flour around the edge of the pie to seal.

7. Place pie on low shelf in the oven. Bake at 425°F (220°C) for 10 to 15 minutes. Reduce heat to 350°F (180°C) and bake for 45 minutes.

8. Remove from oven, cool and enjoy.

Serves 8.

TO FREEZE AND BAKE LATER:

Set unbaked pie carefully in freezer (uncovered) and leave until frozen. Transfer frozen pie to plastic bag and seal tightly. When ready to bake, preheat oven to 425°F (220°C). Remove pie from freezer and brush top with a mixture of 1 tbsp (15 mL) each of milk and sugar. Do not brush the edges as they will burn. Place frozen pie on middle shelf of oven and bake for about 15 to 20 minutes. Reduce oven temperature to 350° or 375°F (180° or 190°C) and bake for about 40 minutes. Watch the crust carefully. If it begins to burn, fit a circle of aluminum foil around the edge of the pie.

LAUREL THATCHER
ULRICH,
A Midwife's Tale,
1991

This Pulitzer Prize winning book brings to life the unforgettable voice of an eighteenth-century midwife and healer and her community in Maine — an intimate portrait of a society at once distinctly different yet similar to our own.

Julie's Lemon Dessert

This incredibly easy recipe balances a creamy texture with a tangy flavour, and can be prepared a day in advance. Julie Cruikshank, the creator of this recipe, is also the editor of a fine collection of life stories told to her by three Native women elders from the Yukon.

2 lemons		
10 oz can	sweetened condensed milk	300 mL
7 oz box	graham wafers	200 g
1/2 cup	whipping cream	125 mL

1. Grate the zest off the lemons and squeeze out juice. Strain juice into a bowl. Add zest and condensed milk, and stir to combine.
2. Place a layer of graham wafers on the bottom of a shallow 2-quart (2-L) glass baking dish. Pour a portion of the lemon mixture on top and spread evenly. Continue to layer wafers and lemon mixture, finishing with wafers.
3. Cool for 24 hours.
4. Two hours before serving, whip the cream and spread over the dessert.

Serves 6 to 8.

A-B-C-D Maple Mousse

This melt-in-your-mouth Canadian dessert is as easy as A-B-C ...
Serve it in demitasse coffee cups with thin butter cookies.

1 tbsp	unflavoured gelatin	15 mL
1/4 cup	cold water	50 mL
3/4 cup	maple syrup	175 mL
2 cups	whipping cream	500 mL

A. Soften gelatin in cold water.

B. Heat syrup until it is very hot, then stir into gelatin mixture. Continue stirring until gelatin is completely dissolved. Cool.

C. Whip cream until stiff peaks form.

D. Fold cream into cooled maple mixture. Place in individual and chill.

Serves 10 to 12.

Key Lime Pie

This famous dessert celebrates the tart flavour of the key limes from Hemingway country.

4 egg yolks		
10 oz can	sweetened condensed milk	300 mL
1/2 cup	juice of a key lime	125 mL
1/2 tsp	cream of tartar	2 mL
6 egg whites		
1/2 cup	granulated sugar	125 mL
1 baked 9-inch (23-cm) pie shell		

1. Preheat oven to 325°F (170°C).
2. Beat egg yolks until lemon-coloured. Slowly blend in condensed milk. Add lime juice and mix well.
3. Add cream of tartar to egg whites and beat until foamy. Continue to beat, adding sugar 1 tbsp (15 mL) at a time, until stiff peaks form.
4. Fold about 6 tbsp (90 mL) of the meringue into the lime mixture. Pour lime filling into pie shell.
5. Top with remaining meringue and bake until golden brown.

Serves 8.

MARGARET FORSTER,
Lady's Maid,
1990

This beautifully written love story of poets Robert and Elizabeth Browning seen through the eyes of Elizabeth Wilson, a lady's maid, is a skillful and readable blend of fact and fiction that draws the reader into a Victorian world full of passion and melodrama. It is a captivating, compelling account of their lives.

Afterword

YOUR BOOK CLUB IS LAUNCHED

LITERARY EXCURSIONS AND GROUP CELEBRATIONS

Among many fine evenings of discussion, there is one especially memorable night when we critiqued cookbooks. One selection was a century-old handwritten recipe book kept by a member's grandmother that included a recipe for limed eggs. Another involved a tour in cyberspace. Each book gave us a glimpse into an age — ranging from heavy cream fresh from the separator up to warmed goat cheese on arugula. Attitudes also became apparent, as some books included instructions for setting a table or saving the water from cooking rice — "It's a grand starch for thin curtains, collars and cuffs."

Kate Aitken, a home economist, journalist, broadcaster and cookbook author, was a well-known voice on Canadian radio in the forties and fifties. The third edition of *Kate Aitken's Cook Book* was published in 1964 and priced at $1.00 for the paperback edition. The final chapter included "a practical introduction to the art of homemaking for a young girl," wherein Aitken outlines a course of study for a young girl to follow from age six through to seventeen, accompanied by recipes of increasing difficulty. She ends with the phrase, "Your daughter is launched."

So, too, we hope, will our suggestions help in the launching of your book club. Like us, you will find your own rhythm, your own way of operating and, over time, your own complementary activities and traditions. This chapter contains ideas for extra book club activities and describes some of the traditions that have developed in our club.

In order to widen our horizons, SWIVEL reserves a supplementary date in the spring for a field trip. Finding excursions to suit the group is a major challenge that has been met with destinations ranging from an inspiring and informative guided visit to a historic cemetery to a hilarious pottery-painting session. We have found these excursions to be thought provoking and great fun. The choice of field trips will certainly reflect the idiosyncrasies of your book club.

CEMETERY FIELD TRIP

One perfect evening, in the face of some skepticism from family and friends — "You are going *where?*" — we visited Beechwood, a well-known cemetery in Ottawa. Cemeteries are places of history, of course, and, as we walked and talked, looking at the immensely varied markers, we were introduced to many important men and women — soldiers, poets, entrepreneurs and politicians — who were all, in their own way, architects of Canada. A brief guided tour helped us to connect many of these names to local history. Further exploration on our own reminded us that Beechwood, which was founded in 1873, is a non-denominational burying ground where people of all cultures, races and religions lie side by side. Recently, this cemetery was declared a national historic site and has seen the inauguration of a National Military Cemetery that can accommodate 6,000 graves.

Like many old cemeteries, Beechwood is as beautiful as it is huge, with ancient trees, sculpted gardens, fountains and walkways, all inviting quiet reflection. Only a dinner reservation drew us away from our ramblings.

POTTERY NIGHT

Our field trip to a paint-it-yourself pottery studio did have something to do with books. On the selected evening, we arrived at the studio bearing plates of finger food, proposals for next year's readings and artistic creativity (to greater or lesser degrees). Some of the group were easily able to juggle eating, book-chat and painting, but others (perhaps less sure of our artistic talents) fretted over such significant decisions as plate *versus* pot or aqua *versus* azure. However, by the end of the evening all the food was consumed, a book list for the next year was proposed and our artistic endeavours were lined up for glazing and firing. We had enjoyed a time of laughter, book-chat and camaraderie — sufficient compensation as one of us glumly compared her mud-coloured bowl to the confidently painted objects of her talented colleagues. Oh, those memories of dismal Grade 9 art classes!

A GALLERY VISIT

Our field trips often supplement a reading choice. In this case, we visited the Firestone Collection of Canadian Art (now located at Arts Court in Ottawa) when it was still housed in Mr. Firestone's Ottawa home. We arranged our gallery trip for a month when we knew that members would be especially busy and probably frustrated with overwork — the pleasure of wandering through a space filled with beauty and interest but requiring no preparation helped to balance our lives. You might choose a high-profile downtown gallery or a lesser-known smaller gallery in an outlying area. Of course, the question of accompanying food should never be neglected: a potluck picnic near the gallery will keeps members' culinary skills sharp.

THE GROUP COOKS

One of our favourite field trips was to the home and business of Pam Collacott, a local cooking guru and author. Her establishment is a comfortable log structure with an efficient cooking space and a proper dining table

at which to consume the results. Since it's somewhat in the bush (several kilometres from town), we were pleased to be there before black fly season. In fact, we liked it so much we went back the next year. The menu, composed of Pam's recipes, was chosen in advance. The first year it was Southwestern U.S., the next Spanish. The benefits of meeting in a cooking school were that we didn't shop and we didn't do dishes.

On arrival, we each chose an item to work on (those who didn't get lost on the way had more choice), and proceeded to do so in pairs. While we chatted about recipes, ingredients, chopping and timing, we viewed each other's cooking "style" with interest — having eaten the results for several years. Dinner conversation was somewhat literary. After all, as a book club, we did have to tell our host about what we'd been reading!

OTHER FIELD TRIP SUGGESTIONS

We have highlighted a few field trips that SWIVEL has enjoyed, but the options are endless. A walking tour of the city to investigate landmarks, literary or otherwise, is an interesting way to spend an evening. Some cities offer a Ghost Walk; be prepared to be spooked, especially around Halloween! After reading the latest whodunnit, book club members might practise their investigative skills at a mystery theatre dinner. Food and wine festivals are also good choices that may provide new and exciting recipes for future meetings. If club members prefer to remain closer to their literary ties, a book selection might be chosen to coincide with a visit from an author. Local authors might also be willing to attend a club evening or the club might choose to hear an author speak in a larger forum.

In addition to our field trips, SWIVEL has developed three strong traditions.

THE GARDEN PARTY

Our last meeting before the summer hiatus is a garden party. The spectacular and well-tended garden of one of our members provides a delightful setting in which we mark significant events of the past year: weddings, milestone birthdays, retirements and book launches are celebrated and savoured. One of the most appealing aspects of a successful book club is the sense of community. The common thread that brought us together — the love of reading — has been transformed into a fabric of affection and caring. In the world outside SWIVEL, some of us are closer friends than others, but we have all become a part of each other's lives in a special and significant way.

SILLY HATS

Perhaps the silliest of our traditions — or is it merely a bad habit? — is the creation and wearing of hats on special occasions. Any teacher who has sat in a meeting has undoubtedly heard a principal, department head or colleague say, "Now let me put on my parent's hat" or "the premier's hat" or "the custodian's hat." One year our creator of invitations offered the challenge of decorating a hat suitable for the annual garden tour and an upcoming wedding that would also serve as a sun shade for the approaching summer vacation. Creative juices flowed and, though most were burdened with end-of-year tasks, the results were extravagant and hilarious. The dictum became "We must do this again next year."

The next year, we each decorated a chef's hat for another member (whose name was inscribed on the brim). Another year, photographs of members were set into emerald patterns and artistically attached to a Burger King crown template. Every once in a while, after an evening of animated discussion, someone says, "Now, we should have been wearing suitable hats."

CHRISTMAS EXTRAVAGANZA

Gatherings in mid-December have always been important social events. Although the ingredients — the people, the food, the music and the traditions — vary from culture to culture, there is a shared sentimentality. For SWIVEL, it is the unique setting of our Christmas gathering that kindles our joy. We gather at Nancy's Christmas Workshop, where ...

> The paintings are hung on the walls with care,
> Depicting all that means Christmas with flair;
> The Christmas poinsettias are blooming bright,
> And yes, that is a Christmas pickle fork to your right!
> The fireplace is transformed into a hearth of angels,
> And everything that is not pinned down jingles and
> jangles!

Most importantly, where else would we hear "We Wish You a Merry Christmas" quacked by a singing and somewhat rhythmic goose? There are some traditions that just make sense!

... but the very last word must go to our pets.

FROM UNDER THE TABLE:
A PET'S VIEW OF BOOK CLUB NIGHT

"No one appreciates the very special genius
of your conversation as a dog does."

CHRISTOPHER MORLEY

This may explain why spouses, partners and children are sent out of the home or relegated to the basement on book club nights, while pets are welcomed. Over the years our pets have provided much impromptu entertainment. There was the night when Parkin, an English Cocker Spaniel, reacted to loud and prolonged laughter during our discussion by throwing back his head and singing with extraordinary gusto. And the night when Jack, a Jack Russell Terrier, ran through the room bouncing a balloon off his nose, travelling faster and bouncing higher as the applause increased. By contrast, Jack's companion Lilly viewed our arrival with resignation. "I can get through this evening," she seemed to say. "I'll just lie here quietly and eventually these people will leave." McKenzie, a Cairn Terrier, sees book club night as an opportunity to get extra petting, constantly nudging reluctant members to comply. Poppy, a Lakeland Terrier, is renowned for her display of figure eights on the lawn of our June garden party. Like Jack, she travels so fast that she is just a blur among the flower beds. The less active pets make their presence felt as well. Toy Poodle Madison looks benign but insists on guarding his chair and ottoman by growling at whoever comes near.

And then there are the cats! Radcliffe, who one evening revealed a fondness for stockings by nibbling on someone's toes for what seemed like an eternity, and Tonner and Grumps who sometimes pass judgement on "the genius of conversation" by simply disappearing.

The dog opened one eye, cocked it at me, and rolled it up before her lids closed. People should not feed moralistic animals. If they're so holy, where are their books?

ANNIE DILLARD
THE WRITING LIFE,
1989

RECIPE SOURCES

Asparagus and Prosciutto
Adapted from LEAF/FAEJ, *Just the Best: Favourite Recipes from Canada's Top Food Writers*, 1992

Avocado & Grapefruit Salad with Poppy Seed Dressing
Adapted from *Sunset Cookbook of Favourite Recipes*, 1968

Bread & Butter Pickles
Adapted from Joanne Lesem, *The Pleasures of Preserving and Pickling*, 1975

Bread Pudding with Whiskey Sauce
From Pam Collacott, *The Best of New Wave Cooking*, 1992

Brie with Mango Chutney & Pecans
Adapted from Fare for Friends Foundation, *Good Friends Cookbook*, 1991

Broccoli Salad
Adapted from Fare for Friends Foundation, *Good Friends Cookbook*, 1991.

Chicken Dijon
Adapted from Anne Lindsay, *Smart Cooking*, 1996

Chicken Marbella en la Calle
Adapted from Julie Rosso and Sheila Lukins, *The Silver Palate Cookbook*, 1988

Chocolate Angel Food Cake
Adapted from Bonnie Stern, *Simply Heart Smart Cooking*, 1994

Coquilles St.-Jacques
Adapted from Government of Canada, *Shell Fish a Plenty*, 1978

Curried Broccoli & Shrimp Salad
Adapted from *The Joy of Microwaving*, 1986

Curried Lamb
Adapted from the Canadian Home Economics Association, *Laura Secord Canadian Cookbook*, 1976

Double Chocolate Bombe
Adapted from General Foods, *Bakers Chocolate Recipes*, nd

Elderflower Pancakes
Adapted from R. Hemphill, *Herbs for All Seasons*, 1972

Ginger Sesame Eggplant Dip
Adapted from Bonnie Stern, *Heart Smart Cooking for Family & Friends*, 2000

Gingered Oranges
Adapted from Barbara Kafka, *The Microwave Gourmet Healthstyle Cookbook*, 1989

Ham & Cauliflower Supper Dish
Adapted from Anne Lindsay, *Light Hearted Cookbook*, 1988

Hawaiian Chicken
Adapted from Janet and Greta Podleski, *Looneyspoons*, 1996

Johnny Cake
Adapted from Edna Staebler, *Food That Really Schmecks*, 1968

Lamb Stuffed with Spinach, Mint and Tomatoes
Adapted from Fare for Friends Foundation, *Good Friends Cookbook*, 1991

Lemon Apple Salad
Adapted from Better Homes and Gardens, *So Good With Fruit*, 1967

Lemon Curd
From Pam Collacott, *The Best of New Wave Cooking*, 1992

Meat Loaf en Croûte
Adapted from Hope Dunton, *From the Hearth: Recipes from the World of 18th Century Louisbourg*, 1986

Mushroom Turnovers
Adapted from Naomi Arbit and Jane Turner, *Ideal Easy Appetizers*, nd

Oatmeal Cookies
Adapted from Edna Staebler, *More Food That Really Schmecks*, 1979

Orange Hummus
  Adapted from Mollie Katzen, *The Enchanted Broccoli Forest,*
  1982

Peach Chutney
  Adapted from *Bernadin Guide to Home Preserving,* 1990

Pork With Apples & Sweet Potatoes
  Adapted from Fare for Friends Foundation, *Good Friends
  Cookbook,* 1991

Raspberry Supreme Torte
  Adapted from Karen Whiteside and Brigitte White, *Be My
  Guest,* 1985

Rhubarb Cordial
  Adapted from *Bernadin Guide to Home Preserving,* 1990

Feta & Bean Salad
  Adapted from Anne Lindsay, *Light Hearted Everyday Cooking,* 1991

Saucy Fudge Pudding
  Adapted from Jean Pare, *Company's Coming—Desserts,* 1986

Savoury Miniature Puffs
  Adapted from Naomi Arbit and Jane Turner, *Ideal Easy
  Appetizers,* nd

Smoked Salmon Mousse
  Adapted from Sharon O'Connor, *The Irish Isle,* 1997

Spanokopita
  Adapted from Mollie Katzen, *The Moosewood Cookbook,* 1992

Strawberry Shortcake
  Adapted from Edna Staebler, *Food That Really Schmecks,* 1968

Turkey Chili
  Adapted from Ellen Brown, *Gourmet Gazelle Cookbook,* 1989

24-Hour Coleslaw
  Adapted from *The Junior League of Indianapolis' Winners,* 1985

INDEX OF RECIPES

INDEX OF AUTHORS